MEN-AT-ARMS SERIES

EDITOR: MARTIN WINDROW

T5-CUL-973

The British Army on Campaign 1816-1902 (3): 1856-1881

Text by MICHAEL BARTHORP

Colour Plates by PIERRE TURNER

OSPREY PUBLISHING LONDON

Published in 1988 by
Osprey Publishing Ltd
Member company of the George Philip Group
59 Grosvenor Street, London, W1X 9DA
© Copyright 1988 Osprey Publishing Ltd
Reprinted 1988, 1989

British Library Cataloguing in Publication Data

Barthorp, Michael
    British army on campaign 1816–1902.—
    (Men-at-arms series; 198).
    3: 1856–1881
    1. Great Britain. *Army*—History
    2. Great Britain—History, Military—
    19th century
    I. Title   II. Series
    355'.00941   UA649

    ISBN 0-85045-835-8

Filmset in Great Britain
Printed through Bookbuilders Ltd. Hong Kong

Artist's Note

Readers may care to note that the original paintings
from which the colour plates in this book were
prepared are available for private sale. All
reproduction copyright whatsoever is retained by the
publisher. All enquiries should be addressed to:
    Pierre Turner
    10 Church Street
    Lyme Regis
    Dorset DT7 3BS
The publishers regret that they can enter into no
correspondence upon this matter.

The British Army on Campaign (3): 1856-1881

Introduction

The third volume of this series sees the Army in a period of reform following the Crimean War (MAA 196). Further changes were derived from the lessons drawn from subsequent European conflicts with which it was not involved. At the same time its main rôle reverted to the security and consolidation of the Empire and its trade, resulting in campaigns large and small all over the world, bearing little resemblance to the conventional European warfare for which the modernising reforms were chiefly designed.

The layout is the same as in the two previous volumes: the campaigns in outline; the methods of the fighting Arms; uniforms, equipment and weapons.

Campaigns 1856-1881

This period was dominated by two major campaigns. At its beginning the almost wholesale mutiny of the Honourable East India Company's

1st European Bengal Fusiliers, in white shirts and trousers, marching to besiege Delhi early in the Indian Mutiny. Lithograph, Capt. Atkinson, Bengal Engineers. (National Army Museum, as are the remainder unless otherwise attributed.)

8th Hussars, in home service undress and covered forage caps, pursuing rebels, Central India 1858. Watercolour, Lieut. J. N. Crealock, 95th.

Bengal Native Army incited other disaffected elements to rebel against British rule. Had this uprising succeeded it would have threatened the validity of the entire British Empire. Its crushing eventually required the presence in the Indian sub-continent of 50 per cent of all the British cavalry and infantry; the deployment there for the first time in the 19th century of the Royal Artillery; and the raising of 26 new infantry battalions at home, and one in Canada.[1] The Queen's troops in India were assisted by all the HEIC European regiments, the loyal regiments of the Madras and Bombay Armies and the Punjab Frontier Force, and new regiments raised primarily in the north-west of India. At its close the Government of India was transferred from the Company to the Crown, the Native Armies were reorganised, and the Company's European regiments were transferred—not without problems—to the British Army.

The end of the period saw a two-year war fought in Afghanistan against the Regular Afghan Army and tribal irregulars. Like the earlier campaign 40 years before (MAA 193), its aim was to ensure that British influence, rather than Russian, prevailed across the North-West Frontier. It involved six cavalry regiments, 38 batteries and 24 battalions of the British Army, and 29 regiments, seven batteries and 71 battalions of the reformed Indian Army.

[1] 2nd Battalions for 2nd–25th Foot, 4th Battalion 60th, 4th Battalion Rifle Brigade; 100th Foot.

Russian expansionism in south-east Europe had been halted by the Crimean War but continued in Asia, leading to the first campaign of the period. The Persian expedition was designed to persuade the Shah to retract his Russian-inspired occupation of Herat, near the southern Afghan-Persian border; its brief course hardly merited its award of four battle honours, though its aim was achieved. The expedition was mounted from India, as were all Chinese operations, and the rescue of the European hostages seized by the Emperor of Abyssinia. All other Indian campaigns of the period were concerned with the suppression of tribal uprisings on the frontiers.

The China Wars were undertaken, in alliance with France, to enforce Chinese observance of treaties over trading rights and treatment of Europeans, made after the 1839–42 war (MAA 193) and subsequently. Another threat to British trade, on the Gold Coast (now Ghana) by the powerful Ashanti tribe, was overcome by Wolseley's expedition of 1873–74. In New Zealand disputes over land rights between colonists and Maoris resulted in further and larger campaigns than the first conflict of 1845–47 (MAA 193).

Across the Atlantic the security of the Canadian border required the deployment of an enlarged British garrison, firstly during the American Civil War after the North's interception of a British ship, and secondly to guard against American-inspired Fenian incursions. The bloodless but arduous Red River Expedition into the Canadian North-West, to punish lawlessness among Franco-Indian half-breeds, saw the last employment on active service of British Regulars in North America, and marked the emergence of Wolseley as a major Victorian military figure.

Towards the end of the period British attempts to federate the various territories in South Africa under the Crown led to the conquest of Zululand, and the revolt of the Transvaal Boers. These were preceded by tribal uprisings on the Eastern Cape Frontier, as had occurred prior to the Crimean War (MAA 193), and in the northern Transvaal. The First Boer War coincided with the completion of another round of military reforms first instituted in 1870 by Edward Cardwell, the War Secretary, as a result of the major European conflict of the period—the Franco-Prussian War.

The campaigns and expeditions are listed below. Against each are shown the battle honours awarded, and the British and HEIC European regiments to whom they were granted. Others present, but not awarded battle honours, are given in brackets, as are those who took part in campaigns for which no honours were awarded. The Royal Artillery and Royal Engineers[1] were never granted individual honours, their universal service being recognised by the motto 'Ubique'. The HEIC Native Armies and post-Mutiny Indian Army are not included. The new designations of the HEIC European cavalry, artillery, engineers and infantry after 1860 are noted after the listed campaigns. Regiments are abbreviated as follows:

British cavalry: Numeral followed by DG (Dragoon Guards); D (Dragoons); LD (Light Dragoons); H (Hussars); L (Lancers).

Royal Artillery/Engineers: RHA, RA/RE.

British infantry: single battalion regiments—64th, 78th etc; two or more battalion regiments—1/5th, 2/9th, 3/RB (Rifle Brigade) etc.

HEIC: B (Bengal); M (Madras); By (Bombay); E (European/s); LC (Light Cavalry); HA (Horse Artillery); FA (Foot Artillery); LI (Light Infantry); F (Fusiliers).

Royal Marines: RMA (Artillery); RMLI (Light Infantry).

King's Dragoon Guards changing Tartar horse at Palichao, China 1860. Drawing, Col. H. H. Crealock.

1856–57 **Persian War.** *Reshire*: ByHA[1], ByFA[1]; 64th, 2nd ByELI[1]. *Bushire*: 64th, 2nd ByELI. *Kooshab*: ByHA, ByFA; 64th, 78th, 2nd ByELI. *Persia*: 14 LD; ByHA, ByFA; 64th, 78th, 2nd ByELI.

1857–59 **Indian Mutiny.** *Delhi*: 6 DG, 9 L; 8th, 52nd, 1/60th, 61st, 75th, 1st EBF, 2nd BEF[1]. *Lucknow*: (Defence (D), Relief (R), Capture (C)): 2 DG(C), 7 H(C), 9 L(R, C); 5th (D, R, C), 8th (R), 10th (C), 20th (C), 23rd (R, C), 32nd (D), 34th (C), 38th (C), 42nd (C), 53rd (R, C), 64th (D), 75th (R), 78th (D, C), 79th (C), 82nd (R), 84th (D, R, C), 90th (D, C), 93rd (R, C), 97th (C), 2/RB (C), 3/RB(C), 1st EBF(C), 1st MEF[1] (D, C); Military Train[2] (C). *Central India*: 8 H, 12 L, 14 LD, 17 L; 71st, 72nd, 80th, 83rd, 86th, 88th, 95th, 3rd ME[1], 3rd ByE[1]. (1 DG, 3 DG, 7 DG, 6 D, 1, 2, 3 BELC[1]; RHA, RA, BHA[1], BFA[1], MHA[1], ByHA, ByFA; RE, B, M, By Engineers; 4th, 6th, 13th, 24th, 27th,

---

[1]Post-1860 designations. 1, 2, 3 BELC = 19 H, 20 H, 21 H (L from 1897). BHA, MHA, ByHA = RHA; BFA, MFA, ByFA = RA. B, M, By Engineers = RE. 1st EBF = 101st; 2nd BEF = 104th; 3rd BELI = 107th; 1st MEF = 102nd; 2nd MELI = 105th; 3rd ME = 108th; 1st ByEF = 103rd; 2nd ByELI = 106th; 3rd ByE = 109th. (Only 1st EBF inverted the word 'European' in its title.)
[2]Successor, from 1857–69, of Land Transport Corps (see MAA 196); elements used as cavalry, hence honours awarded in India and China but not for New Zealand.

[1]After the Crimean War Engineer officers and soldiers of the Royal Sappers and Miners were absorbed into one Corps of Royal Engineers.

2/14th Regiment assaulting the Waikato Pah, New Zealand 1863. Watercolour, Orlando Norie. (West Yorkshire Regiment, on loan NAM)

28th, 29th, 33rd, 35th, 37th, 43rd, RMLI, 51st, 54th, 56th, 2/60th, 3/60th, 66th, 70th, 73rd, 74th, 81st, 87th, 89th, 92nd, 94th, 99th, 3rd BELI[1], 1st ByEF[1], 2nd ByELI.)

1857–60 **Second and Third China Wars.** *Canton (1857)*: 59th. *Taku Forts (1860)*: 1 DG; 2/1st, 1/2nd, 1/3rd, 31st, 44th, 2/60th, 67th; Military Train. *Pekin 1860*: 1 DG; 2/1st, 1/2nd, 2/60th, 67th, 99th; Military Train. (RA; RE; RMA, RMLI.)

1858 **North-West Frontier (Sittana).** (81st, 98th.)

1860–61 **Second Maori War.** *New Zealand*: 1/12th, 2/14th, 40th, 57th, 65th. (RA; RE; RMLI; Military Train.)

1861 **Sikkim Expedition (NE India).** (1/6th.)

1861–62 **Canadian Reinforcement.** (13 H; 1/Grenadier Guards, 2/Scots Fusilier Guards[3], 1/15th, 1/16th, 47th, 63rd, 96th, 1/RB.)

1863–64 **North-West Frontier. (Ambela**: RA; 1/7th, 71st, 93rd, 101st. **Shabkadr**: 7 II; RHA; 79th, 3/RB.)

1863–66 **Third Maori War.** *New Zealand*: 1/12th, 2/14th, 2/18th, 40th, 43rd, 50th,

68th, 70th. (RA; RE; RMLI; Military Train.)

1864 **Japan Expedition.** (RA; RE; 2/20th, RMLI, 67th.)

1865–66 **Bhutan Campaign (NE India).** (RA; 55th, 80th.)

1865–66 **South Arabian Expedition (Aden).** (109th.)

1866 **Fenian Raids, Canada.** (RA; RE; Detachments 2/7th, 1/16th, 2/17th, 1/25th, 30th, 47th, 1/RB, 4/RB, Royal Canadian Rifles[4].)

1867–68 **Abyssinian War.** *Abyssinia*: 3 DG; 1/4th, 26th, 33rd, 45th. (RA; RE.)

1867–68 **North-West Frontier (Black Mountain).** (20 H; RA; 1/6th, 1/19th, 38th, 77th.)

1870 **Canadian Troubles. (Red River**: RA; RE; 1/60th, Royal Canadian Rifles. **Fenian Raid**: RA; Detachments 1/60th, 69th, 1/RB, Royal Canadian Rifles.)

1873–74 **Ashanti War.** *Ashantee*: 2/23rd, 42nd, 2/RB, 1/ and 2/West India.[5] (RA; RE; RMLI.)

1875–76 **Perak Campaign (Malaya).** (RA; 1/3rd, 1/10th, 80th.)

1877–78 **North-West Frontier (Jowakhi).** (RHA; 2/9th, 51st, 4/RB.)

1877–78 **Ninth Kaffir War.** *South Africa 1877–78*:

---

[3]Scots Guards from 1870.

[4]British Army 'local' regiment, 1840–70, formed from older Regulars serving in Canada.

[5]Raised 1795; black soldiers, white officers.

1/13th, 1/24th, 80th, 88th, 90th, 94th. (RA.)

1878–80 **Second Afghan War.** *Ali Masjid*: 10 H; 1/17th, 51st, 81st, 4/RB. *Peiwar Kotal*: 2/8th, 72nd. *Charasiah*: 9 L; 67th, 72nd, 92nd. *Ahmad Khel*: 59th, 2/60th. *Kandahar*: 9 L; 2/7th, 2/60th, 66th, 72nd, 92nd. *Afghanistan 1878–79*: 10 H; 1/17th, 70th, 81st, 4/RB. *Afghanistan 1878–80*: 9 L, 15 H; 1/5th, 2/8th, 1/12th, 51st, 59th, 2/60th, 67th, 72nd, 92nd. *Afghanistan 1879–80*: 6 DG, 8 H; 2/7th, 2/9th, 2/11th, 2/14th, 2/15th, 1/18th, 63rd, 66th, 78th, 85th. (13 H; RHA, RA.)

1879 **Zulu War.** *South Africa 1879*: 1 DG, 17 L; 2/3rd, 2/4th, 1/13th, 2/21st, 1/24th, 2/24th, 57th, 58th, 3/60th, 80th, 88th, 90th, 91st, 94th, 99th. (RA; RE.)

1879 **Sekukini's Revolt (Transvaal).** (RE; 2/21st, 80th, 94th.)

1881 **Transvaal or First Boer War.** (Detachment 1 DG; RA; RE; 2/21st, 58th, 3/60th, 92nd, 94th. Present but not engaged: 6 D, 14 H, 15 H; 2/60th, 83rd, 97th.)

Royal Engineers, Madras Sappers and Miners, and 33rd Regiment storming Magdala, Abyssinia 1868. Watercolour, Capt. Frank James, Bombay Staff Corps.

Fighting Methods

1856–1874

As seen in MAA 196, the Crimean War became—after the early, predominantly infantry battles, in which the British line overcame Russian columns—a siege campaign, dominated by heavy artillery with the infantry consigned to trench warfare, and interspersed with largely fruitless assaults against well-prepared defences. After Balaclava the cavalry had little employment other than outpost duties.

Notwithstanding the major part played by artillery—compared with previous campaigns (see MAA 193)—the improved range and penetration of infantry firearms, and the fact that Inkerman had been won more by small groups of infantry than whole battalions in line, the 'Infantry Manual' of 1857 changed little. The tested evolutions of line and column protected by light infantry extended as skirmishers, and all conducted customarily in 'quick time' of 108 paces to the minute remained unaltered. The standing position remained the norm for loading and firing, whether with volleys or file-firing, though use of cover, kneeling, and even lying down to fire, and 'double time' (150 paces to the minute) were permitted for skirmishers.

Thus, in the open warfare of the **Indian Mutiny**—as opposed to the sieges and defences of cities like Delhi and Lucknow—infantry operated largely as they had in the Crimea and before. Furthermore, they were confronting troops trained in identical methods, so that it was line against line, fought with great ferocity and determination on both sides and inspired by motives ranging from revenge, religion, racial antipathy, resentment and rewards. That in a pitched battle on the plains British infantry could overcome an equal or greater number of sepoy infantry was due in part to inexperienced leadership among Indian officers above company level, but more to the superiority of the British soldier's Enfield rifle—ironically one of the Mutiny's causes—which enabled effective fire to be opened at greater ranges than the sepoy's musket.

92nd Highlanders charging the Afghans at the Battle of Kandahar 1880. Painting, Vereker Hamilton. (Gordon High-landers)

The infantry fighting in defence of, or against the big cities, involved much that was familiar from Sevastopol; watch and ward in the trenches defending the batteries and camps, counter-attacking sallies, storming strongly-held positions, and a new element—street fighting. Amid the jumbled buildings and often narrow roadways, the battalion line had perforce to give way to the column, sometimes with frontages of no more than half-companies, sections or even fours, and most of the work had to be done with the bayonet[1].

Co-incidentally with the mopping-up operations by mobile columns in the Mutiny's closing stages of 1859, the first edition since 1833 of 'Field Exercises and Evolutions of Infantry' was issued. This covered not only the handling of a battalion in the field, but also of higher formations. Though the battalion eight-company organisation remained unchanged (and would continue to do so until 1913), the flank companies were abolished in 1858; and the 1859 manual stipulated for the first time what had already become normal practice: that all infantry battalions must be proficient in light infantry duties, which were defined as protective, reconnaissance, covering and observation. All infantry acting in the light rôle were to be divided into skirmishers, followed, in open country at 200 yards distance, by supports of equal strength and 300 yards behind, by a reserve one-third of the whole; such a force would be 500 yards ahead of the main body deployed in the usual line or column. The intervals would, of course, depend on the nature of the terrain, and advantage was to be taken of cover from fire.

Obviously this greater emphasis on light infantry tactics, or 'Skirmishing' as it was headed in the 1870 edition, was more appropriate for the 400–900 yards range of the Enfield, and the increased rate of fire (10 r.p.m. instead of 2 r.p.m.) of the Snider, the first breech-loader—a converted Enfield. Neverthe-less, the manoeuvres to form line, column, square and echelon in which a main body would deploy continued in force up to the 1870s. The pace for all such movements was accelerated to 110 per minute; double time of 150 paces to the minute was used for charging, rushes, and occasionally for movements of a company within a battalion.

These evolutions were primarily designed with a comparable enemy force in mind, but none of the foes faced by the Army in the 1860s and early 1870s

---

[1]A company was divided into two half-companies, each under a subaltern, and containing two sections commanded by sergeants. Two files made a 'four'.

had disciplined armies in the European sense. All were of varying military sophistication and skill, relying on mass to some degree, backed by weapons ranging from artillery to edged blades. The Chinese and Maoris tended to fight defensively, the former from gun-manned forts or obstacles, the latter from rifle-armed, ingeniously-constructed stockades, or 'pahs'; this continued until the power of modern artillery converted them to guerrilla tactics of raid and ambush. On the North-West Frontier the tribesmen used some long-range sniping, but relied more on a sudden onslaught with edged weapons in mass from ambush or high ground. The Abyssinians depended ultimately on the natural strength of their fortress, Magdala, armed with some primitive guns, but they employed the spear-and-sword charge to delay or attack a vulnerable point. The Ashanti, with slug-filled but lethal firearms, allied their numbers to their thick jungle by forming a loose skirmishing line to attack, chiefly the flanks or rear.

Each required different application of the manual's evolutions, added to powers of endurance to overcome unfamiliar climate and terrain, coupled with high morale to contend with the ferocious practices of foes uncivilised by European standards. Such warfare could require greater decentralisation of command within a battalion than was customary. A weak or weapon-inferior enemy could be brushed aside by skirmishers and supports without even deploying a reserve, let alone a main body. However, many 'small wars' enemies ran away to fight another day; and success depended upon bringing them to battle, cutting their lines of retreat, and crushing them by fire, while at the same time safeguarding the force's vital lines of communication by which casualties were evacuated and supplies and reinforcements brought up. Unlike European warfare, the wounded could never be left to the mercy of the enemy; so their retrieval—like guarding the rear—could be expensive in manpower and effort. The troops needed for such tasks could, depending on the enemy's calibre, be compensated for by having smaller reserves in front.

The assaults on **Chinese** forts and **Maori** pahs saw the storming tactics used at Sevastopol repeated (see MAA 196), though on a smaller scale, and against the Maoris often with as little success:

57th Regiment entrenching a laager, Zululand 1879. 'Graphic' engraving, C. E. Fripp. (Author)

75th Regiment charging in line at Badle-ke-serai near Delhi 1857. Lithograph, Capt. Atkinson, Bengal Engineers.

commanders underestimated their enemy, ordered costly frontal assaults, and failed to block the escape routes. During the advance to Pekin across the North China plain conventional tactics sufficed; an H. H. Crealock eyewitness sketch of an attack shows skirmishers going forward extended, followed by their supports in line, and guns coming into action from a flank in support.

Mountain warfare on the **Frontier** was largely a matter of seizing and holding dominating ground to safeguard a column's advance to destroy a tribal base. During the **Ambela Expedition** of 1863, after the initial approach march, the force became beleaguered in a pass for several weeks while awaiting reinforcements necessary to overcome much stronger opposition than anticipated. The fighting developed into the defence of hill-top picquets, held by one or two companies, against attacks by massed swordsmen supported by matchlock fire by day and night. If a picquet was lost it had to be immediately counter-attacked. Eventually the offensive was resumed, and a formal two-brigade attack on a strongly-held mountain closed the campaign.

In the **Ashanti War** a main column advanced through thick bush and forest on the enemy capital, with three subsidiary and weaker columns on its flanks to divert enemy resources. In such close country, with the constant danger of ambush, a company proved too unwieldy a tactical sub-unit and had to be split into its four, semi-independent sections, three working ahead, the fourth between 40 and 80 yards in rear. When the enemy was encountered in strength, the column would advance in a loosely-formed square, each side of battalion strength, enclosing the headquarters, reserve and baggage; the sides were flexible, each section or company fighting its own little skirmishes but all-round protection being maintained.

After the Crimean War **cavalry** organisation and evolutions remained unchanged (see MAA 196). Throughout this period breech-loading carbines were coming into service, though seldom receiving the training time accorded to sword or lance. The 1869 'Cavalry Regulations' stated that 'attack [i.e. shock action] is its principal object', laying down the attack formation as a first line, arranged in line and mustering one-third of the attacking force; a second of supports, in line or column; and a reserve in column, all at 400-yard intervals. Other cavalry duties—skirmishing, patrols, outposts, advance, flank and rear guards—

received attention but only occupied 5 per cent of the manual.

In the **Mutiny's** early stages a lack of cavalry for pursuit diminished the successes achieved by the infantry. As the cavalry strength built up—ultimately to 15 British regiments—there were plentiful opportunities for attack, often from the flanks or rear while the infantry attacked frontally, against rebel Bengal cavalry, infantry (even breaking their squares) and guns. As the rebel cause weakened cavalry played a major rôle, searching for and hunting down the enemy.

Few British cavalry participated in the other campaigns, which in any case afforded little opportunity for shock action. In **China**, charging in the traditional fashion, the King's Dragoon Guards, had no difficulty routing a horde of Tartar horse, despite the Tartars' habit of shooting from horseback. At Shabkadr, on the **Frontier**, tribesmen were enticed from their heights on to a plain where they were successfully charged three times from a flank by the 7th Hussars, being thrown into such disorder that the infantry, attacking frontally, were able to rout them.

There was, however, need for mounted troops for patrols, outposts, escorts, despatch-riding and guarding lines of communication, as were undertaken in **Abyssinnia** by a squadron of the 3rd Dragoon Guards split up in small detachments. In

Col. Lord Mark Kerr with skirmishing line of 13th Light Infantry at the relief of Azimghur, 1858. Painting, C. A. H. Lutyens. (SUSM)

New Zealand, in default of any Regular cavalry, and before local yeomanry were formed, such work had to be performed by the Military Train, foregoing its logistic function as it had previously done in the Mutiny and China. A cavalry troop was also formed from C/4 Battery RA, which was even called upon to assault dismounted with swords and revolvers at Rangariri Pah.

The adherence to the rebel cause of the Indian-

Squadrons of 7th Hussars in line pursuing rebels in the Indian Mutiny. Drawing, Col. H. H. Crealock.

manned elements of the Bengal Artillery necessi-tated the despatch to India of Royal Artillery horse troops and field batteries to reinforce the HEIC's European **artillery**. Organisation, tactics and armament remained as described in MAA 196. The mutineers handled their guns skilfully, though their reluctance to fight them to the last under attack resulted in gun losses, often to well-handled cavalry supported by horse artillery arriving from an unexpected direction in conjunction with an infantry assault whose way had been paved by field batteries enfilading the enemy position from a flank.

The **Mutiny** was the last major campaign fought with smoothbore guns, with limited range and accuracy largely unchanged since the Napoleonic Wars. The field batteries sent to **China** in 1860 were equipped with Armstrong 12-pdr. rifled breech-loaders (RBL); the same gun and a 6-pdr. version was also used against the Maoris. Firing elongated, instead of spherical projectiles of shell, shrapnel and case with greatly enhanced accuracy and range—more accurate at two miles than a smoothbore equivalent at half a mile—the rifled guns were also lighter, so that a 12-pdr. RBL only required a six-horse gun-team instead of the eight needed for a 9-pdr. SB. The old four-gun, two-howitzer battery armament gave way to six guns in Armstrong-equipped horse troops and field bat-teries.

Notwithstanding the success of rifled guns in action, many batteries had to continue with smoothbore throughout the 1860s, particularly in

Military Train acting as cavalry engaging Maoris at Nukumaru 1865. Watercolour by Gustavus von Tempsky. (Tim Ryan)

India; and the position artillery—18, 24, and 32-pdrs., 8 in. howitzers and 10 in. mortars (see MAA 196)—remained of that type, though a 40-pdr. RBL and even a 110-pdr. had been used in New Zealand, manned by the Royal Navy. Furthermore the breech-loading principle received much criti-cism until, after trials in which the RBLs failed to show to advantage over rifled muzzle-loaders (RML) in range, accuracy and rapidity of fire, it was decided to revert to muzzle-loaders on grounds of simplicity, and cost. From 1871 the 9-pdr. and 16-pdr. RML became the standard field guns for horse and field batteries; their ranges respectively were 2,000–3,300 yards and 1,800–4,000, depend-ing on elevation.

Nor was the improved performance of rifled guns fully appreciated in senior gunnery circles, or the Army generally. Batteries continued to be tied to the cavalry or infantry they were supporting, greater emphasis being placed on gun-drill and alignment at correct intervals from the supported arms, than to tactical deployment best suited to the guns' capabilities. During the Fenian Raids in Canada axle-tree seats were fitted to the 12-pdr. RBLs to give a field battery improved mobility, but generally field gunners still had to march, thus restricting their speed of deployment to the infantry's pace.

This defect mattered less in mountainous or difficult terrain against irregulars, when in any case gunners needed close protection, and when the battery as the fire-unit sometimes had to be broken down to two-gun sections, or even individual guns acting as infantry heavy weapons. Although a horse-drawn field battery of 12-pdr. RBLs accom-panied the **Ambela** and **Abyssinian** expeditions, the guns were soon transferred to elephants, as were 6-pdr. RBLs in **Bhutan** to form an improvised, and the first RA mountain battery; it later went to Abyssinia. The regular Indian-manned mountain batteries at Ambela each had four 3-pdr. SBs and two $4\frac{2}{5}$in. howitzer SBs. Some were converted to rifle-bore for Bhutan and Abyssinia, where two 7-pdr. RML, mule-borne, RA-manned batteries were also used, these guns becoming standard for mountain artillery, with a range of 800–1,700 yards. They also provided the artillery support for the **Ashanti** expedition, used singly or in pairs and manned by Hausas.

7-pdr RML battery, Royal Artillery in Abyssinia 1868. Note mixture of trousers worn with blue frocks.

In general, the campaigns up to the early 1870s were successfully accomplished, sooner or later; but because old habits died hard, particularly among older officers, the new weapons were used for old methods.

1875–1881

The Franco-Prussian War of 1870 made the British Army realise that new weapons required new tactics, or rather a re-adjustment of the old. At the Alma, 16 years before, two **infantry** divisions, supported by another two, had each attacked with all battalions in a single two-deep line. Henceforth attacks would be made in two lines, plus a reserve, but the first line would adopt a formation hitherto confined to skirmishing.

A first-line battalion would attack thus: a fighting line of two companies extended in single rank over some 400 yards and advancing alternately, covering one another with fire; about 180 yards behind, two companies as supports, in whatever formation best suited the ground and the enemy fire, with the tasks of thickening up the fighting line when necessary to maintain the volume of fire, or protecting its flanks; finally, at a 300-yard interval, the main body of four companies, at first in column or quarter-column, later deploying into line, ready to influence the attack as deemed best by the commanding officer.

As the objective was neared, the fighting line would be built up by the supports and ultimately, if necessary, by the main body, possibly from a flank, until fire superiority enabled the whole battalion to advance and finally charge with the bayonet. Double time, as used for the charge, or short rushes

to avoid enemy fire, was increased to 165 paces to the minute, while quick time was also accelerated, first to 116, then to 120 paces per minute. Obviously maintenance of such speeds was affected by the terrain. Suitable cover was to be utilised, but not at the expense of disrupting the attack's cohesion or its line of advance. Furthermore the use of cover and extended order intensified the problem of fire control by officers and NCOs, which the increased rapidity of fire of breech-loading rifles made more than ever essential if ammunition was not to be wasted.

In defence a similar three-tier formation was to be adopted, though the intervals and proportions allocated to each would depend on the extent and nature of the ground to be held. The yardstick for the required density of rifles was that a yard of ground needed three men. Thus a 1,000-strong battalion might be expected to hold a frontage of 300–350 yards, the forward companies perhaps each having three sections in the fighting line with men a yard apart and one section in support, the rear companies being in reserve for counter-attack.

These revised formations, which coincided with the introduction of an improved, but still single-shot breech-loading rifle, the Martini-Henry, were devised for European warfare. However, the chief enemies confronting the infantry after their introduction were the Zulus, Afghans and Boers. The military qualities of the first and last were gravely underestimated; the recently-introduced tactics were imperfectly understood and practised, and against the massed, disciplined but mainly spear-armed Zulus they were inappropriate. One result was the disaster of Isandlwana where, without any fixed defences or obstacles, six companies of the 24th (some 480 men) and some unreliable levies attempted to hold a 1,500-yard frontage—without supports or reserve—against 20,000 Zulus. The same day one 24th company, fighting from behind a barricade, withstood 4,000 Zulus at Rorke's Drift. The lesson was learned: Gingindhlovu was fought from a waggon laager; and at Kambula two battalions (15 companies), six 7-pdrs. and 600 mounted men won the decisive battle of the war, holding a well-sited, all-round defensive position interspersed with quick, local counter-attacks. At Ulundi the Zulu charges were shattered by 33 companies from six battalions and 14 guns in the way that cavalry had been received of old—four-deep, in close order, in square.

The **Afghan War** produced both hill and plains fighting against opposition varying from regular infantry and artillery operating, more or less, in a European fashion, to massed, fanatical charges by largely sword-armed tribal irregular horse and foot. When the Afghan regulars held high ground—as at Ali Masjid, Charasia and Peiwar Kotal—the attack formation worked well, but more rifles could

be allocated to the fighting line and supports since the density and precision of hostile musketry was seldom equal to a European army's; some reserve was always necessary, to guard against flank or rear attack, or to assist the fighting line by enveloping the objective. The nature of the ground and the presence of enemy artillery dictated an extended order and alternate fire-covered rushes in the attack; but instead of designating whole companies as supports, each fighting line company might find its own supports from one, possibly two, of its own four sections, as described above for the defence.

When attacked by massed tribesmen the need was for a dense belt of fire from the maximum number of rifles at maximum range. In the early stages of Maiwand the 66th dealt successfully with such attacks by having all its companies in line along a shallow watercourse, each standing up to fire volleys in turn, initially at 1,200 yards, then lying down to reload and gain protection against enemy artillery and enfilading rifle fire. At Ahmad Khel the 59th also formed a line of companies, but so rapid and enveloping was the enemy rush that the right wing had to be angled back to guard the rear. The tribesmen caught these companies as they were redeploying and the line formation had to be hurriedly converted into company squares which managed to stand firm. Square, of course, gave all-round protection but did not permit the maximum use of rifle-fire obtained from line, and was thus a

Hausa-manned 7-pdr RML protected by 42nd Highlanders, Ashanti 1874. Watercolour, Orlando Norie.

A fighting line with supports (Punjab Infantry) positioned behind laagered waggons and an abattis in defence of the Sherpur Cantonment, Kabul 1879.

last resort at close quarters if the rush had not been broken up by volleys at longer ranges.

Section or company volleys were customarily used at ranges over 600 yards, firing starting from right or left of the battalion for the first volley, thereafter companies firing regardless of others. At shorter ranges independent fire was more usual. However, when defending the Sherpur Cantonment at Kabul against mass attacks, the 67th and 92nd did not open fire until the enemy were within 200 yards and then with volleys—with complete success. The frontages held by battalions at Sherpur were about one yard per man.

The 92nd went all through the Afghan War, and the 58th and 3/60th through the latter stages of the Zulu War; yet their collective experience failed them in 1881 against the **Transvaal** Boers who, though belittled by the Staff, proved the most formidable enemies of the period: good shots, skilled in fieldcraft, every man a mounted rifleman with an instinctive understanding of covering movement by fire. Without mounted troops other than a small *ad hoc* force, the infantry might have fared better using the new formations, had they been allowed to do so. The 58th, ordered to take the steep Laing's Nek position with the bayonet, were hurried up the slopes without extending since they were initially in dead ground from the top and control of movement was easier, and were then ordered to charge before they had time to deploy. Suffering heavy casualties

from the intense Boer fire at close range, they could only retreat, using the attack formation in reverse, one company covering another. So little was the Boers' fighting ability appreciated that the 58th, as in all former campaigns, went into action with their Colours—a practice still permitted by the 1877 'Field Exercises'—but never again after Laing's Nek.[1]

To hold their sector of Majuba Hill the 92nd, far from having the recommended three rifles for every yard's frontage, were forced to extend to 12 yards between men—a thin screen which the Boers had no difficulty penetrating. There was a small reserve for counter-attack but, badly organised, it failed in its task. At the Ingogo, in a very exposed position too large for their numbers, the 3/60th were also widely spaced with no supports or reserve; fortunately the Boers did not attack, but their fire proved costly.

The **cavalry** also received a new manual, 'Cavalry Regulations', in 1874. Although their traditional rôle of shock action received due emphasis, with a similar three-tier formation to the infantry, a new departure was the attention paid to scouting, skirmishing, and particularly 'dismoun-

---

[1]Lives were fruitlessly lost trying to save the 24th's Colours after Isandlwana and the 66th's in the débâcle at Maiwand.

3/60th Rifles over-extended under heavy Boer fire at the Ingogo 1881 assisted by 58th mounted infantry. Note exposed field guns. Watercolour by C. E. Fripp. (Royal Green Jackets)

ted service', using the new breech-loading carbines from cover, enclosed country or behind an obstacle, chiefly against enemy cavalry or limbered-up artillery. Nevertheless, regiments with commanding officers prepared to take seriously these less exciting rôles were rare.

One such was the 10th Hussars, which in **Afghanistan** provided one two-troop squadron for well-performed reconnaissance and outpost duties, mounted and dismounted, with the Kurram Field Force. On one occasion, covering a retirement, one troop was dismounted to fire by sections and checked an advance of 5,000 Afghans. At the battle of Futtehabad the same squadron and another troop covered the withdrawal of some guns with dismounted fire; charged with the Guides Cavalry against tribesmen on the flat—the Guides in loose order, the 10th in double rank; pursued them dismounted into the hills; and finally attacked and took a conical hill in dismounted skirmishing order like infantry.

Against overwhelming numbers of tribesmen advancing in loose order near Kabul, part of the 9th Lancers charged in extended order over unsuitable ground and, despite RHA support, got into difficulties and had to retreat, covered by dismounted fire until rescued by infantry. During the siege of Sherpur the 9th found outlying picquets and dismounted patrols on the walls, but came into their own during the pursuit after the final Afghan

assault. Another example of classic cavalry pursuit was the 17th Lancers' charge after the fugitive Zulus at Ulundi. In Afghanistan the 9th found that the rapid change from mounted to dismounted action such warfare required was hampered by the regulation method of carrying their arms, as will be explained later. During Roberts' march from Kabul to Kandahar the 9th's rôle was confined to advance, flank and rear guards, while along the Khyber line of communication the 6th Dragoon Guards and 8th Hussars were entirely employed in small detachments as escorts and road patrols. Against the Boers the much-needed cavalry arrived too late to affect the outcome.

The **artillery's** new RML guns have already been noted. Its most important post-1870 development was the freeing of batteries from the shackles of conformity with the infantry or cavalry they were supporting. Henceforth battery commanders would be told the aim of the movements ordered for a force and allowed to decide the best means to assist it. This new freedom for gunners to determine their own deployment was confirmed by the issue, in 1875, of the 'Manual of Field Artillery Exercise', the first to be devoted to artillery tactics[1]. In addition the fitting of axle-tree seats to all field guns would greatly improve field batteries' mobility. Though gunners would still march occasionally to save the horses, when mounted the Nos. 2 and 3 went on the waggon-limber, 4 and 5 on the gun-limber, 6–9 on the waggon. On going into action Nos. 2 and 3

[1]Previously the Royal Artillery had had to rely on translations of foreign language publications on such subjects.

would transfer to the gun axle-tree seats, No. 7 to the gun-limber. No. 1, or gun detachment commander, was individually mounted as before like RHA gun-numbers.

Following gunners' new independence and the upgrading of their rôle, however, the nature of the fighting in Zululand, with a limited artillery force armed chiefly with light 7-pdr. RMLs and rockets, required the splitting of batteries down to two-gun sections acting, as in the past, as infantry heavy weapons. The later arrival of a 9-pdr. battery and a four-gun Gatling battery saw no change of rôle, and at Ulundi the guns were sited at the corners or in the centre of the square's sides.

At Laing's Nek the failure of the six guns (four 9-pdrs. and two 7-pdrs.), firing at maximum elevation, to neutralise the Boer riflemen through inaccurate fire and stopping too soon was severely felt by the infantry. At the Ingogo the vulnerability of draught-horses and gunners without gun-shields to rifle fire when without cover so impaired the mobility and effectiveness of the guns that they could only be kept in action by drafting infantrymen to serve them.

In Afghanistan, where most horse and field batteries had 9-pdr. RMLs, a few Armstrong 9-pdr. or 12-pdr. RBLs, the artillery was faced by varying and conflicting problems. First, some of the terrain could only be overcome by using mountain batteries (mule-borne), as used exclusively on the Kabul-Kandahar march, but which lacked range and weight of projectile[1]; or by putting field guns on elephants, as did two RHA sections for the flank attack at Peiwar Kotal, but which were slow and vulnerable. Second, the danger of massed and enveloping tribal attacks, which could usually be held with shrapnel and, as the range decreased, with case, required close infantry protection for the guns. Without it, as happened to A/B RHA and G/4 RA at Ahmad Khel, the guns had to retire rapidly before they were overrun. Third, the Afghans fielded a formidable artillery with guns as good, if not better than the British weapons, and whose effect could only be reduced by dispersal and/or cover, both for the guns and their protective infantry—but this in turn was fatal against a tribal

rush. At Maiwand, supporting a mainly infantry force, E/B RHA faced both superior artillery and the threat of mass attacks. Fighting in the open and aligned between two sepoy battalions, E/B was outnumbered and outgunned, and the sepoys broke. E/B fought its guns until almost surrounded and with tribesmen only 15–20 yards away before retiring, but one section was overrun. Only when attacking Afghan regulars, as at Charasia, could guns be employed in the manner urged by the 1875 manual, choosing the best position for counter-battery fire or to assist the infantry forward. It was found, however, that both mountain and field guns lacked lethality against enemy in stone defences or mud-walled villages, who could only be turned out by an infantry assault.

To sum up these last six years: though tactics had caught up with weapons, much irregular warfare required a reversion to earlier methods, and the ensuing tactical problems witnessed one ultimately successful campaign marred by one disaster, an indecisive war marred by another, and a lost war which inevitably contained the seeds of future conflict.

Regulation Uniforms, Equipment & Weapons

Uniforms

Men-at-Arms 196 explained how the skirted tunic, or doublet for Highlanders, replaced the swallow-tailed coatee and short jacket for all branches of the service except the Royal Horse Artillery from 1854. Infantry and lancers had double-breasted tunics; but the former changed to single-breasted in 1856, effective from 1 April 1857, in conformity with other branches. Apart from minor changes to collars, cuffs, shoulder straps, and slight alterations in cut, the tunic remained the full dress garment throughout this period. The infantry, less Rifles, adopted scarlet for all ranks from 1872, replacing the red formerly worn by the rank and file.

Trousers remained as in MAA 196, though the infantry received dark blue serge for summer, retaining white for hot climates until 1861. In 1866

[1]In the war's later stages one battery was equipped with the much-improved 'screw-gun', 2.5-inch RML, with double the range of the 7-pdr.

10th Hussars skirmishing dismounted in Afghanistan 1879. Note horse-holders at left. Anon. engraving. (Author)

Oxford mixture tartan[1], matching the cloth winter trousers, replaced the summer serge. From 1859 black marching leggings were authorised for all infantry 'to be worn at the discretion of Commanding Officers'. Initially these fastened with buttons plus a strap and buckle at the top, but later the buttons gave way to lacing. Highlanders wore kilts, hose, spats and shoes except for the 71st, 72nd, 74th and, from 1864, the 91st, who wore trews.

Regimental facing colours and Highland tartans are listed at the end of this section.

The Crimean practice of reinforcing mounted troops' trousers with leather, i.e. 'booted overalls', became regulation for all mounted duties from 1861 until the introduction of knee boots and pantaloons for such duties in 1871.

The 1855 'French' shako continued in the infantry until it changed in 1861 and again in 1869 to lower and lighter patterns, except for Guards (bearskin caps), Highlanders (feather bonnets except for 71st, 74th and 91st in diced shakos), Fusiliers (sealskin caps from 1866, racoon from 1871), and Rifles (busby from 1873–77). From 1878, following a preference for German rather than French fashions after the Franco-Prussian War, a blue cloth helmet (green for Light Infantry and Rifles) with a spike was adopted. Only the 1855 shako was ever worn on campaign.

Heavy Cavalry retained the 1847 brass helmet until 1871 when a plainer but similarly shaped pattern was approved. Light Dragoons had a lower, French-style shako until converted to Hussars in 1861. Hussar busbies, also worn by RHA, were reduced in height in 1857, and lance caps in 1856. Busbies with slight differences were also worn by the Royal Artillery and Royal Engineers until 1878 when the helmet was adopted, as it was by the Commissariat and Transport—successor to the all-blue uniformed Military Train, which had formerly worn shakos—and other Departmental Corps.

The undress shell or stable jacket, worn in many campaigns covered in MAA 193, was replaced, at first in India from the late 1850s, later at home, by a serge, later kersey frock, sometimes colloquially called a 'jumper', in the traditional colours, cut like a loose tunic with only five buttons in front. At first without, later with regimental facings, it underwent various minor changes throughout this period. White drill clothing was worn in the Indian hot weather, and its shell jacket was also changed for a frock. Forage caps for infantry remained the Kilmarnock, or 'pork-pie' type, though lower from the 1860s. Some Highlanders retained their 'hummle' bonnets, similar to a Kilmarnock, instead of their regulation Glengarry, which itself became universal for all infantry from 1868. Other Arms retained the pill-box type. In hot climates white covers and curtains were issued for both dress and undress headgear; but from 1858 the wearing of covered dress headgear was abolished in India in favour of a sun helmet covered in white cloth with a turban or 'puggaree' rolled round it and an airpipe forming a crest. From 1870 the crested type gave way to another pattern, also white, of a shape resembling the subsequent home service helmet, with a ventilator on top; from 1877 this became universal for all foreign service, not merely India.

Accoutrements

Infantry accoutrements remained initially of the pouch with shoulder belt/knapsack pattern (MAA 196) with bayonet waistbelt; the haversack, formerly an item of 'camp equipage', became a general issue from 1856. The old 60-round pouch (MAA 193, 196) was replaced by a 40-round main pouch plus a 20-round expense pouch on the waistbelt; from 1859 a 50-round main pouch and ten-round expense pouch (also containing an oil bottle and cleaning rag) were substituted.

From 1871 this long-serving but inconvenient system was superseded by the fundamentally different Valise Equipment, in which the weight of

[1]A type of weave, no connection with Highland dress: Oxford mixture was a very dark grey, almost black.

the 70 rounds of ammunition, carried in twin pouches plus a 'ball bag' on the waistbelt, and that of the man's kit contained in a flexible valise rather than the rigid knapsack, was borne primarily on the hips, supported by shoulder braces. The twin pouches were initially black, later buff leather to match the belt and braces[1]. However, it would be at least a decade before all battalions received it. Similar accoutrements were worn by Royal Engineers.

Accoutrements of cavalry and other mounted men—pouch-belts, sword waistbelts with slings, and tubular valise on the horse—remained essentially unchanged (see MAA 138, 196). Light Dragoons and Hussars wore their waistbelts under their tunics. The introduction of breech-loading carbines dispensed with the buff loop and carbine swivel attached to the pouch-belt, and in 1862 a 2ft. 1in. leather bucket for the carbine was approved, to hang from the saddle behind the right leg. Cavalry 20-round pouches underwent minor modifications, according to the firearm being carried, and from 1878 an additional ten-round expense pouch for attachment to the dragoon's waistbelt or lancer's girdle was authorised.

Breech-loaders also obviated the need for cap pouches which, from 1857, had been fastened to the pouch-belt in front for all Arms. Another common item, the mess-tin, remained the D-shaped pattern, though a circular type was approved for mounted troops from 1870. Not until the approval of the Italian Oliver pattern water-bottle for use with the

[1]Details can be found in MAA 107, *British Infantry Equipments 1808–1908*.

Mounted Infantryman, c.1881. An arm employed in South African campaigns that would be increasingly used in default of, or in preference to cavalry in colonial warfare. (See also MAA 193)

Valise Equipment was the long-serving, circular, blue-painted wooden container superseded. There is no evidence of the latter being issued in India, where, from the Mutiny onwards, a soda-water bottle covered in cloth, leather or buckram was used, even after the Oliver type's introduction.

Gunners' accoutrements depended on their rôle

Royal Artillery 9-pdrs RML sited among the infantry in the square at Ulundi 1879. Note gun-teams and limbers behind. Watercolour, Orlando Norie. (Somerset Light Infantry)

and the principle that their primary weapon was the gun, not a small arm. RHA gunners had sword waistbelts with slings, as did mounted men in field batteries, other than drivers, who were normally unarmed. In some batteries on service the latter had an RA gunners' waistbelt with frog for the sword bayonet, the gunners additionally having a 20-round pouch-belt. From 1873 this pouch was transferred to the waistbelt. From 1878 only gunners mounted on the limber had the 20-round pouch—for the two carbines per gun strapped to that vehicle.

The only accoutrements authorised for officers of all Arms was the sword waistbelt with slings (Highlanders having shoulder belts with slings and a dirk waistbelt) and for mounted Arms, the pouch-belt. However, this was insufficient for field service, for which the following were additionally recommended to be carried on the person: revolver with ammunition, telescope or binoculars, haversack, clasp knife, drinking cup, memo book, watch, and waterproof coat (all of which an officer had to purchase for himself).

Weapons

The infantry's weapon in 1856 was the percussion Enfield (RML) with 39 in.-long barrel, .577 in. calibre, weighing 8lb 14½oz, sighted to 1,200 yards, with a 17 in. socket bayonet. Sergeants and Rifles had a 6 in. shorter and 10 oz lighter version, sighted to 1,000 yards, with a 22¾ in. sword bayonet. These rifles were converted, from 1866, to become the first breech-loaders on the Snider principle firing brass cartridges, with the same lengths and bayonets but 6½oz lighter, and both sighted to 1,000 yards. The Snider was only a stop-gap, and from 1874 the Martini-Henry was introduced: 33 in. barrel, .45 in. calibre, weighing 8lb 10½oz, sighted to 1,450 yards, with a 22 in. socket bayonet, sword-type for sergeants and Rifles. Though still a single-loader, it had an improved rate of fire of 12 rounds per minute over the Snider's ten. It was the last rifle to use black powder which emitted smoke; was prone to jamming and barrel-fouling; and had a vicious recoil—all disadvantageous against the foes encountered latterly in this period.

From 1855 several breech-loading carbines were

Uniforms 1855–70, from left: Infantry 1855, Light Dragoon 1858, RA gunner 1857, Officer Royal Engineers 1864, Lancer 1858, Officers Rifle Brigade, Infantry, RHA 1864, (Two Volunteers), 2nd Life Guards, Infantry bandsman 1870, Coldstream Guards, Hussars, Infantry 1870. Watercolour, R. Simkin. (Author)

tested as replacements for the muzzle-loading Victoria (see MAA 196), including the Terry and the American Sharps; but the .45 in. Westley-Richards, 20 in. barrel, weighing 6lb 8oz and sighted to 800 yards, was eventually chosen and issued from 1866. However, it was quickly superseded by the .577 in. Snider, $21\frac{5}{8}$ in. barrel, weighing 6lb $9\frac{1}{2}$oz and sighted to 600 yards. This remained the regulation cavalry firearm until the issue of the Martini-Henry carbine from 1877: .45 in. calibre, 21 in. barrel, weighing 7lb 8oz and sighted to 1,000 yards. The overall length of all three carbines averaged 36 inches.

The Royal Engineers' .577 in., 3ft $11\frac{1}{2}$ in.-long Lancaster carbine (RML) with 24 in. sword bayonet was also converted to the Snider BL principle from 1866, with a weight of 8lb $3\frac{1}{2}$oz; the same conversion was applied to the shorter and lighter (3ft 4 in. and 7lb $7\frac{3}{4}$oz) Royal Artillery carbine with 23 in. sword bayonet. When the Martini-Henry entered service, the Engineers adopted the rifle and the Artillery the carbine, slightly modified to take a $25\frac{3}{4}$ in. sword bayonet.

In 1868 the regulation 9ft lance with ash stave was replaced by a bamboo pattern.

The 1853 universal cavalry soldiers' sword with three-bar guard continued in service, until it received a new sheet steel guard pierced with a Maltese cross in 1864. The steel scabbard was wood-lined to prevent blunting. The same swords were carried by individually mounted ranks of the Military Train (sergeants, trumpeters, farriers and armourers), and by the RHA and mounted men of field batteries (excluding drivers) until 1876, when they reverted to the 1853 guard. Cavalry officers' swords remained unchanged from the 1821, three-bar guard, Light Cavalry pattern, also carried by RHA, RA and Military Train officers, and steel scroll-pattern guard for Heavies.

Infantry officers continued with the 1845 sword with 1822 guard, which was also used by Engineer officers until 1857 when they adopted a brass, honeysuckle pattern guard, with brass scabbard for field officers, steel for others. From 1866 steel scabbards replaced the old black leather type of infantry company officers. Highland officers had the 1828 steel, basket-hilted broadsword, some regiments having an alternating undress hilt with plain cross-bar guard. Infantry sergeant-majors and staff sergeants had brass-hilted officers' swords, such Highland ranks' broadswords being cast-iron hilted, as were their pipers', drummers' and bandsmen's though with a $2\frac{2}{3}$ in. shorter blade until

Uniforms 1871–81, from left: Rifle Brigade, Dragoon Guards, Highlanders, Infantry, Lancer, all 1874; Officers, Fusiliers, Infantry 1881, (behind) Dragoon Guards (foreign service 1881. Watercolour, R. Simkin. (Author)

1871, when they received 12$\frac{1}{8}$ in. bladed dirks. From 1856 infantry drummers and buglers (Light Infantry and Rifles) received a 19 in. bladed sword with cruciform hilt in brass and iron respectively, bandsmen being similarly armed. Finally, also dating from 1856 was the 22$\frac{1}{2}$ in. bladed pioneers' sword with brass, stirrup-guarded hilt. All non-commissioned infantry ranks' swords had black leather scabbards with brass mounts.

Thus in outline the clothing, equipment and weapons of the fighting Arms as prescribed by regulations. As in the past these made no distinction between peace and war, and very little between conditions on home and foreign service, the latter offering a wide variety of climates and terrain. Yet the campaigns of the period were as much battles against those elements, and the frequent diseases therefrom, as against the enemy—particularly as the Army's post-Crimean recruits were no longer predominantly drawn from the British or Irish countryside, but increasingly from the urban poor, whose physique on joining left much to be desired. That they fought, and usually won, under arduous conditions against superior numbers and often savage foes, says much for the regiments that moulded them into soldiers, and something for the methods and the weapons employed. Also affecting

their performance were the sometimes adverse, sometimes beneficial ways in which the regulation dress was modified for war, as will now be discussed, using such documentary and pictorial evidence as has survived.

Campaign Modifications

Persia and India

The regiments in the Persian Expedition went from Bombay but returned to Calcutta to become immediately involved in the first relief of Lucknow. The Persian operations occurred in the cold season, which had some sunny days but very cold nights and heavy rainstorms. There is little evidence of dress; but an infantryman, either of the 64th or 2nd Bombay Europeans, appears in a forage cap with cover and curtain, shell jacket and winter trousers in a sketch by Capt. Hunt, 78th. A reconstruction of a 78th Highlander is our Plate A1; curiously the 78th, unlike other Highlanders, did not adopt spats until 1858 and, after a particularly punishing march in Persia, their hose and Highland shoes were in such disrepair that they had to be temporarily issued with grey stockings and boots.

Earlier Indian campaigns (MAA 193) had been fought in the cold season, but the Mutiny fighting went on through the heat and monsoon, producing a variety of costume. The 78th had to endure in their thick doublets until after the first relief of Lucknow when lighter clothing was obtained, giving them 'a most motley appearance, dressed like the English regiments'.

A popular garment was the smock-frock, issued for wear on board ship[1], worn by the 5th Fusiliers (Plate A3) and Madras Fusiliers at Lucknow, the 79th in Rohilkand, and the 72nd and 95th in Central India. On leaving England for China the 90th and 93rd had been issued with 'boat-coats' (see Plate C1); diverted to India, some of the 90th wore them at Lucknow, and the 93rd throughout the Mutiny with kilts and feather bonnets to which a quilted sunshade was attached. The bonnet tails gave some protection from the sun and were also worn by the 79th at Bareilly. Many regiments simply fought in shirt-sleeves, a practice then so

[1]See also MAA 193. Plate H2.

unusual as to merit comment in contemporary accounts, e.g. of the 10th, 64th and Bengal Fusiliers.

Regiments stationed in India at the Mutiny's outbreak had their white clothing. At Delhi the 52nd, followed by the 61st, copied a practice first started by the Corps of Guides in 1846 of staining their whites and shirts to a subfusc hue by immersion in mud, tea, coffee, curry-powder or coloured inks to introduce *khaki* (dust-coloured) into the British service, the result ranging from dark grey through slate, light brown to off-white and even lavender (Plates A2, B2). Their example was followed by the whole Delhi force (except the 9th Lancers, who fought in white until resuming their blue uniforms in the cold weather), and spread to other areas of operations, all sorts of jackets, blouses and loose frocks being made up in shades of khaki. In some regiments blue dungaree trousers, much used in campaigns before 1854, provided an alternative to white. Forage caps, with or without covers, were swathed in turbans, and varieties of sun helmet were adopted by some officers (Plate A2). In the fighting's later stages helmets were provided for the men: the 5th Fusiliers, for example, were sketched by Col. H. H. Crealock in May 1858 in airpipe helmets with khaki frocks and trousers—a change from their September 1857 costume at A3, having reverted to their red tunics during the cold weather.

Home service clothing, tunics or shell jackets, was much used in the winter months. Though India-based, the 6th Dragoon Guards fought in their blue

From top: Enfield rifled musket, socket bayonet and scabbard, Short Enfield (Sergeants and Rifles), sword bayonet and scabbard. Snider conversion for Enfield. From equipment manuals. (Author)

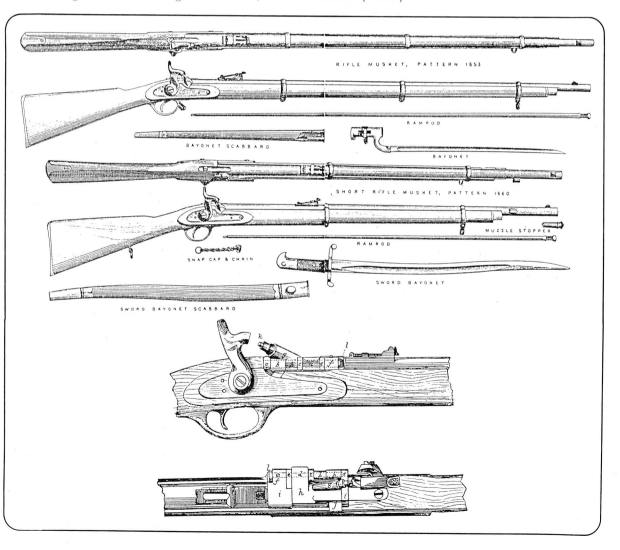

Light Dragoons uniform with brass helmets throughout both seasons, but later dispensed with the helmets (Plate B3). In Central India the 8th Hussars marched in blue stable jackets and booted overalls with covered forage caps. Many of the reinforcing regiments hurriedly sent to India had no time to acquire lighter clothing (Plate B1), and the traditional colours were much in evidence at the capture of Lucknow in March 1858, including the 2nd Dragoon Guards in brass helmets and red tunics, RHA in blue dress jackets with turban-wrapped forage caps, and the 2nd Rifle Brigade in rifle-green. When it grew hotter the latter adopted 'dust-coloured linen with black facings', and for the rest of 1858 most regiments, including those from England, acquired more suitable clothing. The 7th Hussars, for example, wore forage caps swathed in turbans, loose dust-coloured frocks and booted overalls, the 14th Light Dragoons using a similar costume but with only turbans as headdress. The 71st HLI had a lavender-coloured twill suit of

78th Highlander 'dressed like the English regiments' and (behind) 90th Light Infantryman in boat-coat after the first relief of Lucknow, 1857. Watercolour, Lieut. Sankey, Madras Engineers. (India Office Library)

blouse and trousers with wicker helmets in the same cloth.

Sketches by Lt. Upton, 72nd, disclose how a non-garrison battalion's dress developed. They started the Central India campaign in feather bonnets, doublets and trews as though on home service; the bonnets gave way to white-covered and curtained 'hummle' bonnets, which were later dyed, and finally worn with dyed smock-frocks, the trews remaining constant throughout. The India-based Bengal Fusiliers progressed from white, to dyed white, to blue frocks, red tunics, and finally to slate-coloured jean blouses.

China

Despite the widespread use of loose khaki clothing in the Mutiny, it was not adopted generally for service. In the 1857–58 Chinese campaign the 59th wore the afore-mentioned 'boat-coats' in hot weather (Plate C1). At the attack on Canton in December 1857 Crealock sketched gunners in blue tunics with covered and curtained caps. Similar headdress with peaks were worn by the Royal Marines with blue serge frocks at White Cloud Mountain and when landing against the Peiho forts in June 1859, their officers having helmets.

There is no evidence of boat-coats in the 1860 campaign. For the landing on 1 August the force General Orders stipulated 'cloth trousers [Oxford mixture], summer frocks [red serge] and wicker [airpipe] helmets', though the 2nd Division ordered serge trousers [blue]. Each man was to have 56 rounds of ammunition, greatcoat folded with mess-tin attached, water-bottles and haversacks containing three days' rations. Once ashore and on the march men were to carry their knapsacks with greatcoats folded flat at the back; those regiments possessing waterproof sheets were to roll them 'horse-collar fashion' round the knapsacks. When actually in action, as at the Taku Forts, knapsacks were set aside, as was customary in colonial campaigning when they were normally transported. Officers, not having knapsacks, carried their greatcoats or capes 'en banderole' on the march, and there is evidence that some preferred forage caps to helmets (Plate C2). Crealock's sketches confirm this dress for the infantry and show the King's Dragoon Guards in brass, plume-less helmets with turbans or, probably later in the

Persia & India, 1857:
1: Private, 78th Highlanders
2: Officer, 1st European Bengal Fusiliers
3: Corporal, 5th Fusiliers

A

India, 1858:
1: Private, 97th Regt.
2: Officer, Bengal Horse Artillery
3: Private, 6th Dragoon Guards

B

China:
1: Private, 59th Regt., 1858
2: Field Officer, 99th Regt., 1860
3: Driver, Royal Artillery, 1860

C

1: Pte., 40th Regt.; New Zealand, 1863
2: Sgt., 71st HLI; Ambela, 1863
3: Pte., 2nd Bn., 7th Royal Fusiliers; Canada, 1866

D

Africa:
1: Pte., 33rd Regt.; Abyssinia, 1868
2: L/Cpl., Royal Engineers; Abyssinia, 1868
3: Sgt., 2nd Bn., Rifle Bde.; Ashanti, 1874

E

Afghanistan:
1: Pte., 67th Regt., 1879
2: Officer, 72nd Highlanders, 1879
3: Pte., 9th Lancers, 1880

F

Afghanistan:
1: L/Cpl., 59th Regt., 1879
2: Officer, 66th Regt., 1880
3: BSM, Royal Horse Artillery, 1880

G

South Africa:
1: Cpl., 3rd Bn., 60th Rifles, 1879, 1881
2: Officer, 58th Regt., 1879, 1881
3: Pte., 92nd Highlanders, 1881

H

campaign, airpipe helmets, tunics and booted overalls or, for officers, long boots pulled on over their trousers. He depicted a field battery dressed as in Plate C3 but with its commander wearing a frock fastened with loops and olivets (a popular fashion in the Mutiny), long boots and his sword belt under the frock.

New Zealand

The Maori Wars of the 1860s differed in dress from other contemporary campaigns and the 1845–47 war (MAA 193). Instead of scarlet or red the infantry wore either a blue, shirt-like smock of flannel or serge, or a frock of the Indian pattern in dark blue serge, the better to merge with the undergrowth; both were worn with forage caps and Oxford mixture trousers. Some regiments—e.g. the 43rd, 57th and 68th—wore the 1859 pattern leggings, others following the Crimean fashion of rolling the trousers up or tucking them into their socks (Plate D1) because of the mud.

The blue smock can be seen in the photograph (page 37) of Lt. Waller, 57th. The 68th's officers wore a plain, five-button blue frock; but the 1/12th's, though blue, had concealed buttons with black braid all round and four pointed-end, flat braid loops across the front and a rounded braid figure on the cuffs—a type also worn by Military Train officers, according to the Prussian watercolourist and soldier of fortune, Gustavus von Tempsky, who made many pictures of those campaigns. A variation on this frock, or 'patrol jacket' as it was later called, was that worn by the 50th's officers fastened by loops and olivets. Some officers

95th Regiment in Central India 1858 in ragged smock-frocks, dungaree trousers and native sandals with turbanned forage caps. Watercolour, Lieut. J. N. Crealock, 95th. (Sherwood Foresters)

acquired knee boots of various designs for field use.

Besides their usual belts, haversacks and water-bottles, the men carried greatcoats or blankets and, if in possession, waterproof sheets 'en banderole' with the mess-tin or a pannikin attached. An alternative method of carrying the greatcoat was to roll it up from top to bottom, instead of lengthwise, leaving the sleeves outside to be tied together over the chest, as in Plate E1.

A watercolour by Lt. Robley of his 68th waiting to attack the Gate Pah has two officers with

Bombay Horse Artillery in covered dress helmets and stable jackets with 72nd Highlanders in smock-frocks and trews, Rajputana Field Force, 1858. Watercolour, possibly Lieut. J. N. Crealock, 95th.

9th Lancers in white undress attacking mutineers at Delhi 1857. Lithograph, Capt. Atkinson, Bengal Engineers.

greatcoats 'en banderole' and haversacks; sword belts were usually worn under frocks, though this was impractical for carrying a revolver unless the holster had a shoulder strap (see Lt. Waller).

RA, RE and the Military Train were dressed similarly to the infantry but distinguished by their respective forage cap bands and matching trouser stripes: red, yellow, white; gold (RA, RE) and white (MT) piping for officers' and senior NCOs' caps. The gunners acting as cavalry found sling sword belts unsatisfactory and fastened their scabbards to the saddle instead. Their revolvers were carried in holsters attached to the waistbelts with a strap from the trigger guard securing them to the body. The Military Train acting as cavalry, as depicted by von Tempsky, are accoutred with sling sword belt and pouch-belt with carbine swivel; he gives them light grey-blue trousers, which is at variance with their regulation dark blue.

Indian Frontier

Numerous Indian frontier campaigns occurred in the 1860s for which the red serge frock was the customary service garment rather than any khaki clothing. A detachment of the 42nd, ordered from Peshawar to Kohat in 1867, were to pack serge frocks in their kitbags and march in 'blouse tunics', but their nature is uncertain. Pictorial records of the Ambela expedition show frocks worn by the 71st, 93rd and 101st with, respectively, trews, kilts and serge trousers, airpipe helmets (the 71st's with a red puggaree) or forage caps (Plate D2). The sketchbook of Capt. Howard, 71st, indicated that once operations became static caps were worn exclusively and, when on picquet, equipment was reduced to pouch and waistbelts. The 71st's officers, sergeant-major and bugle-major, whose caps were green, diced and with peaks, suspended their broadswords—with simple cross-bar guards—from sling belts under their frocks, but the dirk, when carried, hung from a black waistbelt worn over the frock. Some officers wore short coats over the frock, possibly the Crimean 'bunny' type (see MAA 196). Their trews were either loose like the men's, or tucked into or rolled above high ankle boots laced up the instep; the commanding officer had knee boots like Plate C2. Pipers wore Glengarries with cocks' feathers, green doublets and kilts.

Howard also drew some of the artillery, initially

with airpipe helmets and scarlet puggarees, later pillbox caps, and blue stable jackets. The men apparently have their blue trousers tucked into long boots, which were non-regulation at the time but may possibly be a residue of the jacked boots of the old Bengal Horse Artillery (see MAA 193).

According to Surgeon Rennie of the 80th, that regiment went up to Bhutan in 1864 with a new pattern helmet covered with quilted white calico which he thought 'a decided improvement on the unsightly and cumbrous wicker-work head-dress formerly worn'; whether this still had the airpipe or a simple ventilator is unknown.

Harry Payne painted the 7th Hussars' charge at Shabkadr with officers in airpipe helmets, the men in peaked, covered and curtained forage caps, and all in home service stable jackets and booted overalls. It was, however, painted nearly 50 years after the event when memories of survivors, if he sought them, may have been less reliable.

Canada

Regulation dress with forage caps was worn for internal security in Canada with the addition, when necessary, of winter clothing: fur caps, gloves and long boots. Plate D3 shows one example, of the 2/7th. His officers had double-breasted greatcoats with light grey astrakhan collars, cuffs, and edging down the front which was fastened with loops and olivets. In a photograph the 78th are similarly dressed to D3 but with a tall, fore-and-aft fur cap with the bonnet badge on the left side for the men, an officer having a round fur cap with turned-up front and side flaps.

Photographs of the 30th in temperate weather,

ready to protect communications from the Fenians show the men in tunics and forage caps, carrying full marching order with blankets rolled on top of the knapsacks, greatcoats either folded flat against the back or 'en banderole'. An officer wears a yellow-faced scarlet frock with concealed buttons, sword belt underneath, and greatcoat 'en banderole'.

On the Red River Expedition the 60th Rifles wore forage caps, serge frocks, trousers and buff moccasins. Most of the time, however, was spent in boats, all ranks, according to Capt. Young, wearing flannel shirts with sleeves rolled up, 'dirty duck trousers and a straw hat or red woollen night cap to crown it all'.

Africa

The Abyssinian Expedition of 1868 was recorded by the eyewitness watercolours of Capt. James, a staff officer, and the cameras of 10th Coy., Royal Engineers. Because the troops faced extremes of climate, both tropical clothing and serge uniforms were needed. For the former the white drill frocks and trousers were dyed khaki before leaving India; this, according to James, was more grey than brown, but obviously varied owing to primitive and unfast dyes. This alternated with red (blue for RA) serge frocks according to brigade orders; both blue and khaki trousers were worn with the serges. 10th Coy. RE, coming from England, did not have white drill but was issued with duck frocks and trousers to supplement their serge clothing (Plates E1 and E2.)

Infantry and Staff advancing across paddy fields, China 1860. Compare men's airpipe helmets with officers'. Drawing, Col. H. H. Crealock.

All were in helmets, the men's of the airpipe pattern, officers generally having a more modern type with ventilator dome.

James shows the 45th on the march and the RE storming Magdala in red, but the 33rd at the latter in grey, as confirmed by orders for the assault. Photographs of the 4th, after the fall of Magdala, show the same clothing, an officer in a dyed white patrol jacket of the type described above for the 50th in New Zealand. RE officers wore a similar blue jacket. Besides their belts, 60 rounds, haversacks and water-bottles (of the Indian pattern), each soldier had to carry his blanket, waterproof sheet and greatcoat; officers had the last three transported for them. G. A. Henty, then acting as a war correspondent, observed that the greatcoats were slung by the sleeves, as described earlier.

The Ashanti Expedition was the first for which a campaign dress was specifically designed, rather than the makeshift costumes adopted hitherto. *The Illustrated London News* of 18 October 1873 described its frock and trousers as made of 'Elcho grey tweed, in which [the troops] much resemble the London Scottish Volunteers. The tunic [sic] introduces a novelty into the uniform of the army in the shape of outside pockets, one on each hip and one on the breast. The garment fits loosely about the neck and

chest, it is confined at the waist by a belt of its own material and there is no stiffness in the collar'. The suit was worn with canvas leggings, slightly longer than the regulation black type, and the 'new pattern helmet, mainly composed of cork and canvas, weighing a little over six ounces, and provided with an inner isolated cone to fit the head, outside of which there is a space for ventilation, further ensured by a perforation at the top'. Wolseley himself specified the helmet's colour should be 'khakee brown'; after the campaign he commented that the suit's colour was 'too light for a dense forest'. Each soldier received two frocks and one pair of trousers of tweed, and one pair of duck trousers (Plate E3). The 42nd had to relinquish their kilts and hose, but retained small scarlet hackles in their helmets. During the heat of the day men were permitted to march in their flannel shirts, slinging their frocks through the waistbelts behind.

This was the first campaign in which the new Valise Equipment was used, though its braces were dispensed with and valises and greatcoats transported. All three battalions were armed with Sniders and a special sword bayonet, the Elcho, with $20\frac{3}{4}$ in. saw-backed blade with swelling spear point.

Wolseley recommended that all officers should carry this bayonet instead of their swords, together with 'a stout canvas haversack', a water-bottle 'as obtained at Silvers and Co., Cornhill', telescope or racing glasses, watch, compass, pocket filter, clasp knife with tweezers. For clothing he suggested 'a

General Cameron (fifth from right, hands in pockets) with Royal Artillery before attacking the Gate Pah, New Zealand, 29 April 1864. (Tim Ryan)

Norfolk jacket, pantaloons and gaiters of strong brown canvas and shooting boots', plus 'strong serge patrol jacket and trousers for use at night'. Curiously his list omitted a revolver, but the Rifle Brigade's colonel reminded his officers of this necessity, also recommending double-barrelled shotguns. The 42nd's officers carried Snider carbines as well as Elcho bayonets. That officers' kit was recommended, rather than ordered, reveals how equipping themselves suitably for service was at private, not public expense.

Afghanistan

The notion of a special campaigning dress was not pursued after the Ashanti War, so regiments in India on the outbreak of the Afghan War still only had their white drill for summer, and scarlet, blue or green serge for winter, the white helmet with puggaree being worn throughout. Furthermore the serge frock was no longer the loose, easy garment of the 1860s but had been smartened up, as in India it was worn as much for parade as the tunic was at home. Neither dress was ideal for a rigorous campaign in Afghanistan, where climatic extremes were to be expected. Regiments again had to devise more serviceable clothing.

Common to all was the fitting of khaki covers over the helmets. For hot weather the white drill was dyed in the bazaars, but this would be inadequate for the cold in which the campaign started. Photographs show that some regiments acquired a khaki frock, on Norfolk jacket lines, seemingly of serge or similar material. At Peiwar Kotal, with the Kurram Field Force, the 8th wore such frocks for warmth over their scarlet serges and the home service trousers. The following winter at Kabul the 67th wore a similar kit, with or without scarlet frocks underneath depending on the temperature (Plate F1). Whereas the 8th had worn their trousers loose, the 67th adopted puttees (from a Hindi word meaning bandages) to support and protect the leg, as worn by Indian troops and soon widespread among the British. Pictorial evidence suggests, however, that puttees were not necessarily worn at all times.

According to Ian Hamilton, the 92nd only had their white drill frocks boiled in tea-leaves to put on over their serges in the winter, wearing their kilts, hose and spats in all seasons (Plate H3). The 72nd

Lieut. W. de W. Waller, 57th Regiment in New Zealand campaign dress of blue blouse. Note shoulder holster. (Tim Ryan)

also retained their tartan trews, officers binding theirs with matching tartan puttees (Plate E2). Whether their men had such puttees is less certain: the accompanying photograph shows officers with them but the men with trews loose. However, a sketch by Sgt. Anderson of the regiment puts the men in puttees, but it is unclear whether these were tartan or plain khaki. This sketch also shows ten cartridge loops sewn diagonally across the front of the khaki frocks for immediate access to ammunition[1].

The 72nd and 92nd were among several regiments still equipped with the old accoutrements, the Valise Equipment being not yet universal in India. When greatcoats were carried they had to be rolled 'en banderole', whereas regiments with the new equipment, like the 67th,

[1]See the author's *The North-West Frontier: 1839–1947* (1982), page 79.

93rd Highlanders in 'hummle' bonnets and red frocks guarding prisoners, Ambela 1863.

carried them folded flat and secured across the shoulders with the straps provided.

Other regiments known to have had the old accoutrements were the 1/17th, 63rd and 59th. The latter, according to sketches by one of its officers, Lt. Irwin, took the field in late 1878 without any khaki, wearing scarlet serges, and were still so dressed in October 1879 (Plate G1). However, by Ahmad Khel the following April it was in khaki.

Irwin's sketches are the only eyewitness evidence discovered so far of scarlet actually being worn on operations in this war. A photograph of the 2/7th Royal Fusiliers on guard at Kandahar shows them in uncovered white helmets with spikes and a grenade badge, scarlet serges, dark trousers and puttees. Other photographs of the 72nd and 92nd in garrison at Kabul reveal Highland frocks and even dress doublets with Glengarries, but such photographs seem to have been taken during lulls in operations. When troops again took the field it would appear, from other pictorial evidence, that some form of khaki was resumed.

The 1/17th, which not only had the obsolete equipment but the old serge frocks with flapped pocket, dyed its white drill by immersing it in mud. A photograph of the Peshawar Valley Field Force contains men who may be of this regiment in this makeshift khaki with puttees. Maj. Hone of the 4th Rifle Brigade, with the same force, recalled that his men's dyed drill was so soiled 'by the perspiration of

the men, the blacking from the belts and the bad dye that we looked a very dirty crowd'.

Regiments with Valise Equipment seem mostly to have had the black leather pouches rather than the buff. A photograph of the 66th parading in early 1880 in scarlet frocks shows black pouches, and those used by a soldier at Maiwand still exist in the Regimental Museum[1]. At that ill-fated battle, fought in the heat of July, the 66th were in khaki clothing with darker brown puttees for the men, bluish-grey for officers (Plate G2). The 8th's pouches were buff, but of the same pattern as the black, with the flap covering the whole front of the pouch and fastening underneath, rather than the buff type used in the Zulu War which fastened on the front.

E/B Battery RHA features in paintings of Maiwand by G. D. Giles, who received details from survivors, and R. Caton Woodville, wearing khaki drill with blue puttees (Plate G3). Officers and senior NCOs of F/A RHA were photographed at Kabul in the winter 1879–80 in slightly different and longer khaki frocks with three open pockets and self-material belt, worn with blue pantaloons and knee boots. G/3 RA appears in photographs in blue serge and khaki drill short 4-button frocks like E/B's, with loose blue or drill trousers except mounted ranks in knee boots.

The 9th Lancers took a variety of clothing to Afghanistan from dress tunics (Plate F3), blue serges, drill frocks like F/A RHA's, and a khaki

[1]At Salisbury (Duke of Edinburgh's Royal Regiment).

38

double-breasted jacket of quilted material, all worn with blue pantaloons and either knee boots or ankle boots with khaki puttees. Home service pantaloons were also worn by the 6th Dragoon Guards and 10th Hussars, either with knee boots or blue puttees, more common than khaki among mounted troops. The 10th had blue serges with them but in action wore khaki frocks, their officers having a special regimental pattern with concealed buttons, flapped breast pockets, and cuffs closed at the wrist.

The defect of the cavalryman's accoutrements (mentioned earlier) was that while the sword hung from the waistbelt slings, his carbine in its bucket was attached to the saddle, which was inefficient for dismounted action. After seeing the 9th at Kabul tripping over their trailing swords or unable to withdraw carbines from under fallen horses, Roberts authorised the carbine being slung across the man's back and the sword fastened to the saddle.

Officers' problems of carrying sword and revolver had been assisted by Gen. Sir Sam Browne's invention of a leather belt to support both weapons (Plate F2). In the opening stages of the war only general and staff officers had such belts; but officers of all Arms who had gone into Afghanistan with only regulation sling sword belts were soon beseeching their friends back in India to send them up Sam Browne belts which, by the end of hostilities, were almost universal and would, in time, be adopted by officers of armies all over the world (as indeed would puttees, the other invention of this war).

Towards the end of the war a means of producing permanently dyed khaki drill was devised in India. Troops in the field received suits of this material, an improvement with important implications for the future.

South Africa
Though the Afghan War had been fought in a variety of costumes, khaki of one sort or another had predominated. However, the three South African

Gen. Sir R. Napier, Force Commander Abyssinia, with Royal Engineers officers in blue patrol jackets, most with non-regulation breeches and boots; booted overalls on right.

Officers, 67th Regiment, Kabul 1879. Note Norfolk jacket type frocks, scarlet frock (centre) and left-hand figure with Sam Browne and rolled greatcoat.

Officers and men 72nd Highlanders in fighting dress, Afghanistan 1879, with old equipment and rolled greatcoats. Officers with tartan puttees, men without.

campaigns fought, more or less, contemporaneously were undertaken in home service undress clothing. Varieties of Sam Browne belts appeared latterly, worn more by staff than regimental officers, but puttees remained an Indian fashion, infantry wearing leggings. Apart from equipment and weapons, the only item common with Indian fighting was the white foreign service helmet, though without a puggaree and usually dyed brown.

A more uniform appearance prevailed in the last of the Kaffir wars on the eastern Cape frontier in 1877–78 than in the campaigns there 25–30 years before (see MAA 193). W. W. Lloyd of the 24th sketched his men in helmets and scarlet serges, though one has the brown trousers, another the wideawake hat of the earlier wars. The Martini-

G/3 battery, Royal Artillery, Afghanistan 1880, in khaki drill with 9-pdr RML. Mounted officers and men in knee boots.

Henry was first used in action in this campaign by the 24th and 90th, though British battalions had it throughout the Afghan War.

The infantry of both Zulu[1] and Transvaal Wars, some of whom fought in both, wore scarlet frocks with Oxford mixture trousers and leggings, except the 3/60th in black serge (Plate H1) and the 91st in the Highland frock and trews of Government tartan with a red line. Some frocks had facing colour patches on both collars and cuffs, e.g. the 21st, 24th and 94th; others only on the collars, e.g. 3rd, 80th and 90th.

All had Valise Equipment, most with buff pouches though the 1/13th, 91st and of course 3/60th had black; the 94th had both types. As in India the valises were usually transported, but greatcoats were strapped across the shoulders on the march, except in the 91st who carried them 'en

banderole'. Men detached as mounted infantry[2] had 60-round bandoliers, and some wore corduroy trousers instead of the regulation pattern, with leggings.

Officers wore either the 1872, so-called 'India-pattern' (after being abolished for home use in 1874) scarlet frock or patrol jacket, with collar in the facing colour, piped all round with white, and rank shown by a system of Russia braid on the cuffs (Plate H2); or the black-braided blue patrol jacket with olivets, authorised from 1867 as the official replacement for the shell jacket. Legwear varied, including regulation trousers, pantaloons or cord breeches with knee boots or leggings, either the men's or a higher pattern fastened with buttons; the 91st's officers all had calf-high boots laced up the instep.

[1]See also MAA 57.
[2]This Arm will be further discussed in Vol. 4 of this series.

41

Officers, 10th Hussars, Afghanistan 1879, in regimental pattern khaki frocks and home service nether wear. Note Sam Brownes worn with dress pouch-belts. (R. G. Harris)

The Artillery and Engineers dressed as the infantry in blue or scarlet serges, though some photographs show gunners in tunics or blue Guernseys. The 17th Lancers in the Zulu War appear to have retained their double-breasted tunics but buttoned over to show blue instead of white, with pantaloons and knee boots.

The only exception to traditionally coloured clothing in these campaigns was in the 92nd Highlanders who, despatched straight from India for the Transvaal War, arrived in their Indian khaki drill and obsolete equipment, exactly as they had fought in Afghanistan (Plate H3). Thus khaki came to Africa; but, as will be seen in the next volume, this did not yet signify the end of traditional colours for campaigning in that continent.

* * *

Regimental Facing Colours up to 1881

Scarlet/Red Tunics

Blue: 1 LG, 2 LG; KDG, 4 DG, 1 RD, 2 D, 16 L; RE; Grenadier, Coldstream, Scots Gds; 1st, 2nd, 4th, 6th, 7th, 8th, 13th, 18th, 21st, 23rd, 25th, 35th, 42nd, 50th, 51st, 79th (from 1873), 85th, 86th, 87th, 100th, 101st, 102nd, 103rd, 104th.

Buff: 2 DG (cream); 3rd, 14th, 22nd, 27th, 31st, 40th, 48th, 52nd, 61st, 62nd, 71st, 78th, 81st, 90th, 105th.

Green: (Dark) 5 DG; 68th, 73rd, 79th (until 1873). (Gosling) 5th. (Lincoln) 11th, 45th, 49th, 55th, 63rd, 69th, 94th. (Grass) 19th, 24th, 36th, 39th, 54th, 66th.

Yellow: 3 DG, 6 D; 9th, 10th, 12th, 15th, 16th, 20th, 26th, 28th, 29th, 30th, 34th, 37th, 38th, 44th, 46th, 57th, 67th, 72nd, 75th, 77th, 80th, 82nd, 83rd, 84th, 88th, 91st, 92nd, 93rd, 95th, 96th, 99th, 108th.

White: 17th, 32nd, 41st, 43rd, 47th, 59th, 65th, 74th, 98th, 106th, 107th, 109th.

Scarlet/Red: 33rd, 53rd, 76th.

Black: 7 DG; 58th, 64th, 70th, 89th.

Purple: 56th.

Sky-blue: 97th.

Blue Tunics

Scarlet: RHG; 3 LD[1]/H, 4 LD[1], 5 L, 9 L, 12 L, 14 LD[1]; RHA, RA; Ordnance (various titles 1856–81).

Buff: 13 LD[1]/H.

[1]Converted to Hussars 1861.

White: 6 DG, 17 L; Military Train/Commissariat and Transport.
Blue: 4 H (from 1861), 7 H, 8 H, 10 H, 11 H², 14 H (from 1861), 15 H, 18 H, 19 H, 20 H, 21 H.
Black: Army Medical Staff.
Green Tunics
Scarlet: 60th.
Black: Rifle Brigade.

Highland Regimental Tartans

Kilts
42nd, 93rd: Government.
78th: Government, red/white lines (Mackenzie).
79th: Cameron of Erracht.
92nd: Government, yellow line (Gordon).
Trews
71st: As 78th.
72nd: Prince Charles Edward Stuart.
74th: Government, white line.
91st: Government, red line.³

²Crimson trousers.
³From 1864, formerly uniformed as English infantry.

9th Lancers at Kabul 1880 showing variety of uniforms worn: dress tunics, stable jackets, serge frocks and quilted winter jackets.

The Plates

A: Persia, India 1857
1: Private, 78th Highlanders
2: Officer, 1st European Bengal Fusiliers
3: Corporal, 5th Fusiliers
According to officers' recollections, the 78th (**A1**) fought its way to Lucknow in the winter clothing it had used in Persia, less feather bonnets which had been left at its Poona barracks before departure for Persia, covered 'hummle' bonnets being worn in lieu. Single-breasted doublets having not yet been issued, the first pattern was still in use. For hose and shoes, see 'Campaign Modifications' chapter. In Persia blanket and greatcoat were carried in the knapsack straps; and he has the 40-round main pouch and 20-round expense pouch with the Enfield rifle.

A2 is based on the Bengal Engineer G. F. Atkinson's Delhi lithographs in which 1st EBF frequently features. He wears his dyed white shell jacket and trousers in the relaxed manner common at the siege, and a helmet with extensive puggaree. His men fought in covered forage caps and shirt-sleeves, thereby earning their regimental nickname, 'The Dirty Shirts'. An undress waistbelt suspends his 1822-hilted sword, a cummerbund supports his revolver.

The smock-frock and trousers of **A3**, as worn at the first relief of Lucknow, are as recollected by Cpl. Bishop. Smock-frocks were also cut up to make covers and curtains for the forage caps, to which were affixed peaks removed from their unused shakos. Besides belts and pouches as for A1, he carries a haversack and Enfield rifle. His cap pouch is on his pouch belt, A1's in his doublet.

B: India 1858
1: Private, 97th Regiment
2: Officer, Bengal Horse Artillery
3: Private, 6th Dragoon Guards
According to Lt. Safford the recently-arrived 97th marched to Lucknow in early 1858 in home service tunics, summer trousers and covered 1855 shakos, less ball-tufts, as in **B1**, but changed their shakos for covered forage caps during its capture in March. Officers had four-button scarlet frocks, with regimental facings on collars and pointed cuffs, instead of tunics; immediately afterwards they obtained loose white drill frocks and trousers.

3rd Buffs with Zulu prisoners 1879. Note red frocks with buff collar patches, trefoil on cuffs, home service trousers with leggings, Valise Equipment, no helmet puggarees. (Local History Museum, Durban)

In dyed white drill stable jacket and trousers with non-regulation boots of a type common among officers in the Mutiny, **B2** is based on a Crealock sketch of Bareilly, fought in May 1858. BHA Dress Regulations specified brown leather sword belts in undress. His gunners had dyed white booted overalls. This battery, 2/1, had left Meerut for Delhi in May 1857 in their laced blue jackets (see MAA 193), hacking off the red collars with jack-knives, and changing to white during the siege.

Also based on Crealock, **B3** wears the cap adopted after the brass helmets (worn at Delhi) were set aside, and the Light Dragoons dress peculiar to this regiment and adhered to throughout the fiercest Mutiny fighting. He has slung his tunic through his pouch-belt. The carbine is the Victoria but some cavalry, e.g. 8th Hussars, had the Sharps (BL). Sword: 1853 universal cavalry pattern.

C: China
1: Private, 59th Regiment, 1858
2: Field Officer, 99th Regiment, 1860
3: Driver, Royal Artillery, 1860
Based on a photograph and descriptions, **C1** wears the red-faced, holland boat-coat issued for the 1857

Royal Artillery in Zululand with 9-pdr RML. Most are in blue serge, some in Guernseys. (Africana Museum Johannesburg)

China Expedition (in which only the 59th participated, its other battalions being diverted to the Mutiny) for use on the rivers, and summer serge trousers. Crealock shows RA and the 59th attacking Canton with greatcoats and blankets carried thus. Note cap pouch in the slit pocket above the expense pouch, not on the pouch-belt. Pouches as in Plate A.

C2 is based on a photograph. Note 1855 pattern forage cap and this regiment's officer's frock, worn with non-regulation breeches and boots and the cape portion of the greatcoat. Many infantry officers adopted pouch-belts to carry field glasses or revolver ammunition during the Crimean War. 1822-hilted sword with field officer's brass scabbard.

Based on a Crealock drawing of the attack on the Taku Forts, **C3** shows the airpipe helmet, worn by all Arms, tunic and booted overalls. Drivers were usually unarmed but Crealock shows them with the RA sword bayonet. As drivers rode the near-side draught horses, they required a right leg guard as shown. The numeral below the grenade on the shoulder strap indicates that his battery belonged to 4th RA Brigade.

D: Worldwide, 1860s
1: Private, 40th Regiment, New Zealand, 1863
2: Sergeant, 71st Highland Light Infantry, Ambela, 1863
3: Private, 2nd Battalion 7th Royal Fusiliers, Canada, 1866

Based on photographs and contemporary watercolours, **D1** and **D2** show the serge frock worn respectively against the Maoris and on the North-West Frontier with winter trousers and regimental trews. D2 still has the 1855 expense pouch, D1 the 1859 pattern. The photograph used for D1 shows, additionally to the rolled blanket, the greatcoat carried as in E1. His mess-tin was attached to the blanket, greatcoat or haversack. D2 carries a locally-made (Nowshera) topcoat instead of the regulation greatcoat; his bonnet bears a fir sprig denoting the 71st's marksmen, also shown by his skill-at-arms badge. Helmets were not worn in New Zealand, and were largely discarded at Ambela once operations became static.

In contrast **D3** shows a winter kit for internal security in Canada based on Richard Ebsworth's notes, with the same belts and pouches as D1. The greatcoat had been improved since the Crimea, its cape being deeper over the sleeves, its new stand-and-fall collar having a tab to fasten it when turned up (concealed here by the muffler). The fur cap's grenade came from the Fusilier dress cap.

All three rifles are Enfields, D2 having the sergeants' shorter version with sword bayonet.

E: Africa
1: Private, 33rd Regiment, Abyssinia, 1868
2: Lance-Corporal, Royal Engineers, Abyssinia, 1868
3: Sergeant, 2nd Battalion Rifle Brigade, Ashanti, 1874
E1 and **E2**, based on photographs and Capt. James's watercolours, show the airpipe helmet and mixed dress worn in Abyssinia: E1 in dyed white drill with 1859 pattern leggings, E2 serge and duck trousers. E1's greatcoat has a waterproof sheet tied to it, and he carries the buckram-covered Indian water-bottle. He has the Snider rifle, E2 the

45

Officers, 2/21st R.N.B. Fusiliers in 'India-pattern' frocks, home service trousers, in South Africa.

Lancaster with sword bayonet, both breech-loaders. On occasions the 33rd wore red serges with dyed trousers, and a 10th Co. RE photograph shows some men as in E2, others all in duck clothing.

E3, based on descriptions, wears the new helmet and special Elcho-grey tweed devised for this campaign, but with the alternative duck trousers substituted, and canvas leggings. His Valise Equipment belt and pouches are without supporting braces. Note the Oliver pattern water-bottle issued with this equipment, and the Rifles' black haversack. He has a clasp-knife in his top pocket secured to a button, the Elcho sword bayonet and short Snider prescribed for Rifles.

F: Afghanistan
1: Private, 67th Regiment, 1879
2: Officer, 72nd Highlanders, 1879
3: Private, 9th Lancers, 1880
All three are in winter kit from photographs taken

around Kabul (see 'Campaign Modifications'). **F1** has Valise Equipment, less the valise itself which was always transported. His water-bottle was as E1's, the covered mess-tin is strapped to the back of the waistbelt, and his Glengarry is under the greatcoat straps. The method of tying puttees follows an officer's sketch of a 67th soldier. He has the Martini-Henry rifle and socket bayonet.

F2, based on a photograph of Lt. Egerton, is accoutred with Sam Browne belt, binoculars, revolver, broadsword with undress hilt, rolled greatcoat and privately-ordered water-bottle. For his men, see main text and accompanying photograph. The tartan is Prince Charles Edward Stuart.

F3, based on a photograph of a dismounted sentry, wears an Afghan 'poshteen' of sheepskin over his dress tunic with home service nether wear. He wears no sword belt, only his pouch-belt (see 'Campaign Modifications') and carries a Martini carbine. The quarterings on the forage cap were peculiar to Lancers. Poshteens were much worn by officers of all Arms in the winter.

G: Afghanistan

1: Lance-Corporal, 59th Regiment, 1879

2: Officer, 66th Regiment, 1880

3: Battery-Sergeant-Major, Royal Horse Artillery, 1880

Scarlet serge frocks were not usually worn in action in Afghanistan except as under-garments for extra warmth in the winter; however, two sketches by Lt. Irwin show his regiment operating near Kandahar at a more temperate time of the year as in **G1**. The frock is of a pattern that superseded that in D2. According to Irwin the 59th still had the old equipment.

G2, based on Frank Feller's Maiwand painting, a commemorative tablet advised by an officer, and photographs of 66th officers, is in dyed white drill. Having lost his helmet he has substituted his Glengarry, by now the undress cap for all infantry ranks. The sources show both Sam Brownes and regulation sword belts, as here. The 66th's men had equipment as in F1.

G3 is based on the Maiwand painting by G. D. Giles; he received details from E/B Battery's sergeant-major, who features in the painting. The short four-button frock was peculiar to artillery, the sword belt being worn under it. Lower ranks had red shoulder cords. Though some 9th Lancers' photographs show khaki puttees, dark blue was becoming customary for mounted troops. Water-bottles and haversacks were worn over opposite shoulders to infantry. Sword: 1864 pattern with 1853 hilt.

H: South Africa

1: Corporal, 3rd Battalion 60th Rifles, 1879, 1881

2: Officer, 58th Regiment, 1879, 1881

3: Private, 92nd Highlanders, 1881

Owing to the fugitive nature of rifle-green dye, the frocks and trousers of the 60th were now of black serge. **H1** is based on C. E. Fripp's watercolour of the Ingogo battle against the Boers, which shows a reduced Valise Equipment being worn; Zulu War pictures of this battalion show it complete. Note Rifles' sword bayonet. 60th officers had black Sam Brownes in 1881.

Signallers, 58th Regiment, with heliograph, the chief means of communication used in Afghanistan and South Africa. Their frocks have black collar patches with castle badge. (Africana Museum, Johannesburg)

The 58th Colours carried at Laing's Nek (1881) and in the Zulu War were of the obsolete, 1855 pattern, 6ft by 5ft 6 in.; the Regimental Colour in **H2** is carried by a lieutenant wearing the 'India-pattern' officers' frock (see 'Campaign Modifications') with rank insignia on the cuff. His leggings fasten with buttons instead of laces as in H1. His 1822-hilted sword is hooked up for ease when marching. Note his and H1's helmets without puggarees.

The 92nd at Majuba (**H3**) were in the clothing and obsolete equipment they had used in the Afghan War, carrying rolled blanket, greatcoat and waterproof sheet and three days' rations in haversacks. The 58th, with Valise Equipment (buff pouches) carried the greatcoat etc. in the same way at Majuba. This figure, when compared with the Highlander at A1, illustrates some of the changes in fighting dress over 25 years.

Notes sur les planches en couleur

A1 Uniforme d'hiver tel qu'on le porte en Perse, à l'exception du bonnet de tissu au lieu de la coiffure à plumet de la tenue complète; notez le doublet croisé et désuet; couverture et manteau replié noués dans les courroies du sac de permission. **A2** Veste blanche et pantalon typiques teints localement dans une couleur sombre; et un large *puggaree*. **A3** Un smock-frock et un pantalon portés lors de la délivrance de Lucknow; les smocks sont coupés pour s'en protéger le visage avec des pans retombant sur le cou et portés sous les calots munis de visières prises sur les shakos inutilisés.

B1 Arrivé tout droit d'Angleterre, il porte la tenue de service national sans le plumet et il a couvert son shako de 1855. **B2** Veste d'exercice et pantalon teints en blanc, bottes non réglementaires et calot avec protection matelassée d'après un croquis fait par un témoin à Bareilly. **B3** Hormis le casque de bronze remplacé par un calot, ce régiment a gardé son uniforme de dragons légers pendant toute la mutinerie; également d'après un croquis de Crealock.

C1 Veste en étoffe de 'Hollande' avec distinctions en rouge et pantalon d'été en serge; les sacs sont semblables à l'illustration A. **C2** De même que pour C1, cette reproduction est faite d'après une photographie; calot de 1855 et 'frock', modèle d'officier de ce régiment, porté ici avec des pantalons et des bottes qui ne sont pas réglementaires et la cape du manteau. **C3** Un croquis de Crealock de l'action aux Forts de Taku montre ce costume; notez le casque avec une crête à 'tuyau d'air', porté par tous les hommes de troupe.

D1 D'après des photographies et des peintures: 'frock' en serge et pantalon d'hiver; on ne porta pas de casque en Nouvelle-Zélande. **D2** Le 'frock' à nouveau avec les trews régimentaires; le Nowshera local remplace la capeline. L'écusson sur l'avant-bras et le brin de pin sur le calot dénotent qu'il s'agit des tireurs d'élite de ce régiment. Les casques ont été mis de côté généralement lors des opérations statiques d'Ambela. **D3** Un ensemble local pour l'hiver canadien. La capeline améliorée a une cape plus longue, et (cela est caché par une écharpe ici) une patte pour fermer le col lors des positions debout. L'écusson avec grenade sur le calot vient de celui de la tenue complète des Fusiliers. Sacs comme sur D1; les trois hommes ont des fusils Enfield, D2 porte le modèle plus court pour sergent avec pointe baïonnette.

E1, E2 D'après des photographies et des aquarelles du Capt. James, qui montrent le mélange des tenues portées en Abyssinie: E1 porte des vêtements d'exercice blancs teints en gris olivâtre et des guêtres de 1859, E2 une veste de serge et des pantalons en 'duck'; tous deux ont des casques à tuyau d'air. E1 a une couverture imperméabilisée fixée à sa capeline et une gourde de modèle indien; il porte un fusil se chargeant par la culasse, le Snider, et E2 le Lancaster. **E3** Tweed 'Elcho-grey' créé pour cette campagne mais avec des pantalons en 'duck' et des guêtres de toile; Valise Equipment porté sans les tirants d'épaule; gourde Oliver; musette noir des Rifles; et Snider court.

F1 Valise Equipment sans la Valise elle-même; gamelle couverte à l'arrière de la ceinture; calot Glengarry rentré sous les pattes de la capeline repliée, il est également difficile de le voir, même gourde que E1; fusil Martini-Henry. **F2** Une photographie montrant le Lt. Egerton; notez les bandes molletières apparemment coupées sur de vieux trews, gourde achetée dans le privé, épée avec poignée cruciforme en opalin. **F3** Manteau local, dit *poshteen*, populaire en hiver, porté sur l'uniforme de la tenue complète du service national en Angleterre, à l'exception du calot et de la ceinture pour l'épée qui manque; notez la carabine Martini.

G1 'Frock' en serge écarlate d'un modèle remplaçant celui sur D2, porté très occasionnellement tel quel en Afghanistan mais généralement comme sous-veste en hiver. **G2** Uniforme blanc de 'drill' teint en khaki; le Glengarry est maintenant la coiffure de tous les grades d'infanterie pour la petite tenue, il n'est plus uniquement réservé aux unités écossaises. Notez la ceinture réglementaire pour l'épée au lieu du 'Sam Browne' tout aussi populaire. **G3** Court 'frock' à quatre boutons particulier à l'artillerie; molletières bleues foncées souvent portées par les troupes montées; gourde et musette portées sur l'épaule opposée par rapport à celle de l'infanterie.

H1 'Frock' et pantalon de serge noire: la teinture vert-rifle se détériorerait rapidement sous les tropiques. Notez le Valise Equipment réduit et en noir pour les compagnies de Fusiliers; et l'écusson sur le casque. **H2** Drapeau du régiment, un modèle de 1855, pour le 58ème Regt porté lors de la bataille de Laing's Nek, en 1881. Le porte-drapeau a un 'frock' d'officier le modèle indien, avec insigne de grade sur la manchette; guêtres boutonnées; pas de *puggaree* de casque. **H3** Même tenue à Majuba qu'en Afghanistan. Comparez-la avec le personnage A1 pour l'effet des modifications de l'uniforme de combat au cours des dernières 25 années.

Farbtafeln

A1 Winteruniform, getragen in Persien, ausser dem stoffbespannten Hut anstatt der federgeschmückten Kopfbedeckung. Siehe altes, zweireihiges Doublet; Decke und gefalteter Mantel werden mittle der Riemen des nicht vorhandenen Knapsacks getragen. **A2** Typische weisse Jacke und Hose, örtlich gefärbt in matten Schattierungen; und umfassende Puggaree. **A3** 'Smock-frock' und Hose, getragen beim Entsatz von Lucknow; die Smocks wurden zerschnitten für Feldmützen, die Schirme von unbenutzten Tschakos bekamen.

B1 Frisch aus England, trägt er Inlandsuniform und seinen Tschako von 1855, aber ohne die runde Quaste, dafür mit zusätzlicher Bedeckung. **B2** Gefärbte weisse Stalljacke und Hose, unvorschriftsmässige Stiefel und Kappe mit gesteppter Bespannung—von der Zeichnung eines Augenzeugen bei Bareilly. **B3** Abgesehen vom Messinghelm, ersetzt durch eine Kappe, hat dieses Regiment seine typische Uniform Leichter Dragoner während der ganzen Meuterei beibehalten; auch dies wieder nach einer Crealock-Zeichnung.

C1 'Holland'-Stoffjacke mit roten Markierungen und Sommerhosen aus Serge; Taschen wie in A. **C2** Wie C1, nach einem Foto: Feldmütze von 1855, und der im Offiziersmuster dieses Regiments gehaltene 'Frock', mit unvorschriftsmässigen Breeches und Stiefeln und dem Cape des Wintermantels getragen. **C3** Eine Crealock-Zeichnung von der Taku Forts-Aktion zeigt diese Kleidung; siehe Helm mit durch 'Luftröhren' ventiliertem Kamm, getragen von allen Soldaten.

D1 Nach Fotos und Gemälden: 'Frock' aus Serge und Winterhose; Helme wurden in Neuseeland nicht getragen. **D2** Wieder der 'Frock' mit Trews, den Regimentshosen; anstelle des langen Wintermantels der lokale Nowshera-Mantel. Sowohl Abzeichen am Unterarm als auch Fichtenzweig an der Kappe zeigen Scharfschützen des Regiments an. Helme wurden für statische Operationen bei Ambela meistens nicht getragen. **D3** Lokale Winterausrüstung für Kanada. Der verbesserte lange Wintermantel mit längerem Cape und einer Vorrichtung (hier von Halstuch verdeckt) zur Befestigung des Kragens in aufgestellter Position. Das Granatenabzeichen an der Kappe stammt von der Galauniformkappe der Füsiliere. Taschen wie in D1; alle drei Männer haben Enfield-Gewehre, das kürzere Sergantengewehr (D2) mit Bajonett.

E1, E2 Nach Fotos und den Aquarellen von Capt. James: gemischte Uniformen in Abessinien; E1 hat schmutzigweisse Trainingskleidung und Hosen von 1859, E2 eine Sergejacke und 'Duck'-Hose; beide tragen 'Luftröhren'-Helme. E1 hat eine wasserdichte Stoffbahn an seinem Wintermantel befestigt, und trägt eine Wasserflasche nach indischem Muster; bewaffnet ist er mit einem Snider-Hinterlader, E2 mit einem Lancaster. **E3** Der 'Elcho-grey'-Tweed, bestimmt für diesen Feldzug, aber mit 'Duck'-Hose und Segeltuchgamaschen; Valise Equipment wird ohne Schulterriemen getragen; Oliver-Wasserflasche; der schwarze Brotbeutel der Rifles, und kurzes Snider.

F1 Valise Equipment ohne Valise; Kochgeschirr in Behälter hinten am Gürtel; Glengarry-Kappe unter den Gurten des gefalteten Wintermantels, hier nicht zu sehen, und dieselbe Wasserflasche wie E1; Martini-Henry-gewehr. **F2** Ein Foto zeigt Leutnant Egerton; siehe Wickelgamaschen, offenbar aus alten Trews zugeschnitten, privat erworbene Wasserflasche, Schwert mit Palin-Kreuzgriff. **F3** Lokaler Poshteen-Mantel, beliebt im Winter, über kompletter Ausgehuniform—ausser Feldmütze und Schwertgurt; siehe Martini-Karabiner.

G1 Scharlachroter Serge-'Frock' mit Muster, das auf das in D2 folgte, an sich nur gelegentlich in Afghanistan getragen, sondern meist als Winterunterkleidung. **G2** Weisse Trainingsuniform, auf Khaki gefärbt; die Glengarry-Kappe wurde jetzt von allen Rängen in der Infanterie getragen, nicht nur von den Schotten. Siehe vorschriftsmässigen Schwertgurt anstatt des ebenso beliebten 'Sam Browne'. **G3** Kurzer 'Frock' mit 4 Knöpfen, typisch für Artillerie; dunkelblaue Wickelgamaschen für berittene Truppen; Wasserflaschen und Brotbeutel, von der Infanterie auf beiden Schultern getragen.

H1 Schwarzer Serge-'Frock' und Hose: die Riflegrünfarbe zersetzte sich in den Tropen. Siehe reduziertes Valise Equipment in Rifleschwarz; Helmabzeichen. **H2** 1855 Regimentsflagge des 58. Regiments in der Schlacht von Laing's Nek, 1881. Der Fähnrich trägt den Offiziers-'Frock' in 'India-Muster' mit Rangabzeichen an den Manschetten; Knopfgamaschen; kein Helm-Puggaree. **H3** Dieselbe Uniform bei Majuba wie in Afghanistan. Vergleiche dies mit Abbildung A1, um die starken Veränderungen der Kampfuniform innerhalb von 25 Jahren zu erkennen.